Comprehensive Volleyball Statistics
A Guide for Coaches, Media and Fans
by Stephanie Schleuder

Volleyball Informational Products
Edited by Kinda S. Lenberg

VOLLEYBALL
INFORMATIONAL
PRODUCTS

Published by Volleyball Informational Products
1227 Lake Plaza Drive, Suite B
Colorado Springs, CO 80906
1-800-275-8782
FAX (719) 576-7778
email: cgam@avca.org

Published 1998

Printed in the United States of America.

Cover design by Dennis Kugizaki, Kugizaki Design, Colorado Springs, Colo.
Text design/layout by Kinda S. Lenberg
Front cover photos by Dan Houser

Printed by Gilliland Printing, Inc., Arkansas City, Kan.

Comprehensive volleyball statistics: a guide for coaches, media and fans/Volleyball Informational Products.
    p. cm
    ISBN 0-9665440-0-5 (pbk.)
    Library of Congress Catalog Card Number: 98-61062

Table of Contents

Dedication

This book is dedicated to my mom. Her love, encouragement and support have been a positive, sustaining source of strength throughout my life. I also wish to acknowledge the many players whom I have had the privilege of coaching. These players have taught me more about coaching than any book or mentor. They have shared their emotions, dreams and aspirations and have allowed me to participate in a part of their lives.

Introduction

Coaching as a Profession

Coaching is a complicated and often frustrating job. I also believe it can be one of the most exciting and rewarding professions. There has been much discussion recently about whether coaching is, in fact, a real profession. Groups outside of the coaching ranks that have studied such issues argue that coaching will not likely become an established profession, but the work we do as coaches can be "professionalized" and the occupation can become more established and valued (Chelladurai, 1986). In his paper about coaching, Chelladurai sites several areas which we as coaches need to address in the process he calls professionalization. He lists several significant attributes of a recognized profession which need to be met before it can move from the state of becoming toward the state of being a profession. These include:

•**"Having an organized body of knowledge** - This includes developing special competencies, skills and practice of the profession; generating more knowledge through research and publication of experiences of successful members; developing the special skills and competencies (intellectual and practical) of new entrants through a tough and prolonged training period—usually measured by a specific number of years.

•**Professional authority** - This area deals with the professional being recognized as having the power to decide how and when to provide services to a client (athlete); the use of this power must be limited to the knowledge base accepted and administered in the professional's training and education; the clients must recognize the knowledge base differential between themselves and the professional for any "authority" to exist.

•**Sanction of the community** - For this to occur, the community must accept the ability of the profession to control the training, acceptance and monitoring of its members; the community also prevents non-members from engaging in the activities of the profession; usually the community grants these exclusive rights and privileges to occupations dealing with areas of established social concern and problems of living.

•**A regulative code of ethics** - In order to enhance and legitimatize itself, the profession sets forth a set of beliefs, including its mission and values; further, the profession attempts to [model] the behavior of its members through a code of ethics; professional organizations usually emphasize the values of service, rational behavior and impartial actions" (Chelladurai).

When I review the attributes listed above, I am struck by how far we really have to go before the community as a whole will come to accept coaching as a real profession. However, after looking at the attributes listed, I am also impressed by the progress the national organizations have made toward this end. The sport's National Governing Body (NGB), USA Volleyball, has made significant headway in developing educational programs and instituting practical training for coaches' certification through the Coaching Accreditation Program (CAP) and has recently adopted a Code of Ethics for members of the USAV. The American Volleyball Coaches Association (AVCA) has become an important entity involved in education, advocacy, political action and professional service, adopting and adhering to the tenets of its own Code of Ethics and Conduct, as well. Other organizations on the national scene are taking proactive stances regarding the issues facing education and sport in general, which will serve only to better the sport.

Therefore, the steps of moving from a position where coaching is considered an occupation to the "process of becoming" a profession appears to be in motion. Whether we ever reach the "state of being" seems to be a question which requires too much of a leap, at least right now. I believe that our challenge as coaches is to endorse the programs of our national organizations and become active within them. It would be in our best interest to embody their philosophies, missions and values. If we do not adopt these founding principles, we cannot expect the community to recognize their importance to our society. We have a tremendous amount of expertise within our group. Sharing and working together can benefit us all. Insisting on ethical, professional behavior from our colleagues is an excellent starting point.

Why Use Statistics?

Volleyball coaches have an obligation to learn the basics of collecting and interpreting statistics for the sport. This understanding will not only enhance the ability of coaches to be successful for the players, but will also allow us to inform and educate the media about the intricacies of the sport. When members of the media know the game, they can appreciate the skill level of the players better. The media plays a major role in promoting the sport when they report it in greater detail. Fans of the sport will become more knowledgeable spectators with a little more insight into the ebb and flow of the game. The internet has become a virtual "Monday morning quarterback" site for hashing out the details of matches from all over the country. Match statistics are often an integral part of these on-line discussions. The American Volleyball Coaches Association (AVCA) services volleyball by providing extensive team and individual stats from all levels of play in the United States.

Purpose of the Text

The contents of this book are specifically meant to assist volleyball coaches (and other interested parties) to develop a better understanding about some of the tools which are available to them in the area of statistics. It is laid out to be as user-friendly as possible, with an abundance of easily understood forms and charts which can be adopted for immediate use. In addition, many examples of specific situations are given. Of special interest to the coach are sections outlining statistical ranges for players at varying levels of play. There is information for both novice and more experienced coaches. Interspersed throughout the text are personal opinions about how coaches can interpret and use these statistical methods. A special chapter detailing computer software currently available is also provided. Finally, it is a goal of USA Volleyball and the AVCA to standardize volleyball statistics throughout the country. Hopefully, this text will serve as a vehicle through which this goal can be accomplished.

Acknowledgments

The purpose of this manual is to share some of the knowledge I have accumulated throughout my 23 years of coaching. I have been lucky to have had success as a coach and I attribute this modest accomplishment to the knowledge others have shared with me. Coaching is a people-centered activity whereby success usually depends upon your ability to have a vision, to plan, administer, communicate, teach, evaluate and understand the motivation of those you work with daily. Most of my best "teachers" have not been generally regarded as great coaches or well-known people. They are people who helped teach me some life lessons and shared their insight on understanding human behavior. In my college days, before Title IX, some of my college coaches were, in fact, coerced into coaching. But, no matter how difficult the situation, I have taken away valuable lessons.

Acknowledgment needs to be given to the AVCA and USA Volleyball. Their leaders and members have contributed a great deal to this work. A special acknowledgment must be made to Jim Coleman, general manager of the U.S. national teams, who is responsible for developing many of the statistical concepts discussed in this book. L. Ravi Narasimhan graciously provided his charting tutorial for inclusion in the manual. I also wish to thank all of those who took the time to read the many drafts and give me their valuable feedback. Finally, I wish to thank those who knowingly or unknowingly

shared their knowledge with me. There are countless other methods of using and recording volleyball statistics, but this is a starting point. To begin your adventure into the world of volleyball stats, I would like to share one of my favorite stories, "Lesson From the Geese." A good friend gave this to me many years ago and I have treasured it ever since.

Stephanie Schleuder

Chelladurai, P. (1986). Coach education: a preparation for a profession. *H.R.H. The Princess Anne*, E. & P.N. SPON, University of Western Ontario, 139-150.

Lesson From the Geese

When you see geese flying along in a "V" formation, you might be interested in knowing what scientists have discovered about why they fly that way. It has been learned that as each bird flaps its wings, it creates an uplift for the bird immediately following. By flying in a "V" formation, the whole flock adds at least 71 percent greater flying range than if each bird flew on its own.

Lesson: People who share a common direction and sense of community can get where they are going quicker and easier because they are traveling on the thrust of one another.

Whenever a goose falls out of formation, it suddenly feels the drag and resistance of trying to fly alone and quickly gets back into formation to take advantage of the "lifting power" of the bird immediately in front.

Lesson: It pays to take turns doing the hard tasks, and sharing leadership–with people, as with geese, interdependent with each other.

The geese in formation honk from behind to encourage those up front to keep up their speed.

Lesson: We need to make sure our honking from behind is encouraging–not something less helpful.

Finally, when a goose gets sick or wounded or shot down, two geese drop out of formation and follow it down to help protect it. They stay until the goose is either able to fly again or dies. Then they launch out on their own, with another formation or to catch up with their flock.

Final Lesson: If we have as much sense as the geese, we'll stand by each other as they do.

Author unknown

Stephanie Schleuder

Stephanie Schleuder was an NCAA Division I women's volleyball coach for 23 years, most recently at the University of Minnesota. Schleuder is now the head women's volleyball coach at Macalester College in St. Paul, Minn. She is a charter member of the American Volleyball Coaches Association and has served in several leadership capacities, including vice president, chair of the Awards Committee, chair of the All-American Committee and Division I representative to the Board of Directors. Schleuder is also an active member of the USA Volleyball Coaches Accreditation Program (CAP) Cadre and serves on the Board of Directors for the USAV North Country Region. A successful coach, Schleuder has more than 650 career wins. She is a graduate of the University of Minnesota, Duluth, and earned her master's degree from Bemidji State.

L. Ravi Narasimhan

L. Ravi Narasimhan is presently on the research faculty in the Department of Physics at the University of California at Los Angeles (UCLA). His interests in volleyball are as a spectator. For many years, he has compiled charts at collegiate matches in the United States in an effort to learn the game from the outside looking in. He holds a bachelor's degree in physical chemistry from the University of California at Berkeley and a Ph.D. in that field from Stanford.

Chapter 1

"We are confronted by insurmountable opportunities."
Walt Kelly, author of the comic strip "Pogo."

Serve and Serve Reception Statistics

Most coaches agree that serving and passing are two of the most important aspects of the game. As the skill of the team and individual players improves, passing and serving are not always the most significant factors in determining the eventual winner of a match. However, for most teams, basic passing and serving are critical components to success and will occupy a large portion of each practice session. Coaches can increase the intensity and effectiveness of a player's practice by keeping serve and serve reception statistics during practices, as well as during matches. Use volunteers, managers or injured players to assist with this process. During a match, it is important for the coach to have immediate and direct feedback about a specific player's serving and passing effectiveness. Matches can easily be lost by the failure of a coach to make adjustments when passing and/or serving skills break down. As the season progresses, team and individual efficiency averages will provide the coach with valuable information to help make decisions about specific line-ups and match-ups. Following is one method of evaluating the serve and the pass of the serve. This rating scale, originally developed by Jim Coleman (general manager, U.S. national teams) and Bill Neville (head women's volleyball coach, University of Washington), has been universally adopted in volleyball circles. The same rating scale has proved to be an excellent tool and is still used by the U.S. national teams.

The Rating System
The Serve

The rating scale gives an overall classification of the serve based upon how the opponents pass the serve. This is probably the single best indicator of an individual player's effectiveness in serving because it is dependent upon the skill of the server and the passing ability of the opposition. Each serve is judged and given a point value on a scale of 0 to 4, based on the location of the pass and the resulting options available to the opponent's setter. Following is the rating scale:

- 4 = ace or serve directly resulting in a point;
- 3 = pass by opponents is set by someone other than the setter; the setter has only very limited setting options; or the ball is passed over the net onto the server's side;
- 2 = opponent passes the ball to an area such that no middle attack option is available to the setter;
- 1 = perfect pass by opponents; all setting options available to setter;
- 0 = illegal serve/error.

The Serve Reception (Pass)

The rating scale gives an overall rating of how well an individual player passes the serve. Only the initial pass of the serve is recorded. Subsequent passes of free balls or digs are not included in this area. An aggressive serve puts pressure on the passers to deliver a good pass. Each pass off the serve is rated based upon the end location and trajectory of the pass using a scale of 0 to 4. An ideal pass will allow a setter to choose any setting option, maximizing the potency of the offensive system. In this rating system, a "perfect pass" is recorded as a 3. The trajectory of the pass is as important as the end location of the pass. A pass may be delivered to area 3 (see Figure 1-1), but if it is too flat in its trajectory (low), the setter's only option may be to use a bump-set and hope a hitter can take a swing at the ball. In this case, the passer would receive a "1" even though the pass was directed into area 3. Conversely, if the pass is a "sky ball," it is difficult to set and slows down the pace of the offense. The key in evaluating each pass is to judge the setting options reasonably available to the setter. Following is the rating scale used to evaluate serve reception:

- 4 = this rating is not used for evaluating passing;
- 3 = the passed ball goes directly to the target area and allows the setter all hitting options;
- 2 = the passed ball is directed to an area which does not allow a middle hitting option;
- 1 = the passed ball cannot be played by the setter and/or leaves only very limited setting options or the ball is passed over the net to the serving side;
- 0 = ace—the passed ball and/or attempted pass directly results in a point for the opponent.

Important Note: When taking statistics for passing and serving, the statistician should make sure that the ratings given for a single serve and the resulting pass add up to a total of four points (i.e., if the server gets three points, then the passer must get one point). However, if the server makes a serving error, that

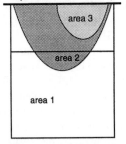

Figure 1-1: Examples of Serve and Serve Reception Evaluation

Area 1: A pass to this area is usually recorded as a 1 and a serve which is passed to this area is usually recorded as a 3.
Area 2: A pass to this area is usually a 2 and a serve which is passed to this area is also recorded as a 2.
Area 3: A pass to this area is usually considered a 3 and a serve which is passed to this area is given a 1.
Over the net: A pass to this area is usually a 1 and a serve which is passed to this area is recorded as a 3.

player is given a 0 and no points are awarded for the opponent's passers.

Figure 1-1 shows the approximate areas used in evaluating serves and serve reception balls. A good, quick setter who can also jump set can effectively expand some of these areas; conversely, a slow-footed setter will diminish the size of the areas. For example, a good setter may be able to get to–and effectively set–a pass in area 1 (shown in Figure 1-1). If this occurs and the setter still has two front-row options (probably the left-front and the right-front hitters), then the pass should be rated a "2" rather than a "1". When these options are not available, the pass should be rated a "1". Note: It is important for the statistician to record the opponent's missed serves (0s) if the coach wishes to compare team passing and serving statistics at the end of a match.

Serve and Serve Reception Situations

•Situation 1: Player A serves the ball over the net and Player B passes the ball at an ideal trajectory to area 3. Player A receives a 1 for the serve and Player B receives a 3 for the pass. If the pass had gone into area 3, but the trajectory of the pass was very flat or too low to allow the setter all setting options, the value of the set would be reduced to either a 2 or 1. The serve would then correspondingly raise in value to a 2 or a 3.

•Situation 2: Player A serves the ball over the net and Player B attempts to pass the ball, but it is shanked off her arms out of play into the bleachers. Player A receives a 4 for the serve and Player B receives a 0 for the pass. Even if someone on Player B's team makes a valiant effort and touches the shanked pass, if the team does not have a reasonable attempt to keep the ball in play, the serve is counted as an ace. The pass is a 0.

•Situation 3: Player A serves the ball over the net and Player B passes it toward the net near area 3, but the ball passes over the net into the opponent's court. Player A receives a 3 for the serve and Player B receives a 1 for the pass. In this situation, the overpass may result in a kill for Player A's team, but Player B still has the pass recorded as a 1.

•Situation 4: Player A serves the ball over the net and the ball drops to the floor between Player B and Player C. Player A receives a 4 for the ace serve. If the statistician cannot determine which player (B or C) should have taken the served ball, a "team reception error" (0) is assessed. (There is an area on the AVCA Official Box Score for recording team reception errors (see page 29).

Recording Options
Practice Pass and Serve Chart - Appendix, Form 1

This chart is useful for recording passing and serving statistics during practice sessions. Assistant coaches, managers, injured players or others can be assigned to tally players' performances for passing and serving. Divide the players up into small groups and assign one person to evaluate the serve and subsequent pass for the group. Figure 1-2 shows an

Figure 1-2: Practice Pass and Serve Organization

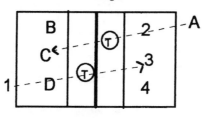

example of organization for passing and serving in practice. Manager 1 would evaluate and record for groups A-D and Manager 2 would evaluate and record for groups 1-4.

Figure 1-3 shows an abbreviated sample of a form used to record passing and serving during practice. The totals

Figure 1-3: Abbreviated Practice Pass and Serve Chart

Player	Serving	Totals	Avg.	Passing	Totals	Avg.
Jackson	231334	16/6	2.67	3221322	15/7	2.14
Thomas	221230	10/6	1.67	331220	11/6	1.83
Klein	432304	16/6	2.67	3332313	18/7	2.57
Bradford	222321	12/6	2	1212032	11/7	1.57
Mattson	22303	10/5	2	221223	12/6	2

and average are calculated at the end of the drill. (Calculations are discussed in the next section.) By having information recorded for immediate feedback, practice sessions usually become more productive and game-like. Players will practice with more attention and motivation when they know that their performance is being recorded. The players know they have an opportunity to make an impression on the coach or to work toward a specific goal. This type of data also gives the coach some reassurance that decisions being made about line-ups are based on facts.

Match Pass and Serve Statistics - Appendix, Form 2

This chart allows the coach to have a snapshot of how each player is passing and serving. Each serve and serve reception is evaluated and recorded in the player's appropriate section of the chart.

There are three columns within the serving and passing area for recording the location where the skill was performed (e.g., right, middle or left areas of the court). The Match Pass and Serve Chart, seen fully as Form 2 in the Appendix, also allows for space to record time-outs, team and individual substitutions, and running score. (Calculations are completed at the end of the match and will be discussed later.)

Figure 1-4 is an abbreviated sample of the chart used to take passing and serving statistics during competition. This chart can be kept easily by one person on the bench during play. It is also advisable to have the same person maintain a similar chart for the opponents, keeping track of good or poor passing and serving. A recommendation would be to have the chart kept by a coach who has responsibility for serving, thereby allowing the coach to make serving recommendations (or call the service areas) for the team. Before the first match of the season, the head coach should outline "triggers" for the statisticians. A trigger is a guideline for the statistician, telling statisticians when they should report player's tendencies to the head coach. For example, if one player misses two straight serves, the statistician should notify the head coach. Another trigger might be if a player has a string of three "1" passes, the statistician will inform the head coach. Conversely, if an opponent is passing poorly, the head coach should also be notified so the serving strategy can be directed at that player. The specific triggers are obviously up to the discretion of the head coach. At the end of a game, the person keeping the passing and serving chart should give the head coach a brief summary of how the team and specific players are passing and serving.

In Figure 1-4, Hammer is not passing well, especially in game No. 2. Hammer's passing in game No. 1 should cause concern and after the first game, the statistician should, at the very least, let

Figure 1-4: Abbreviated Match Pass and Serve Chart - Game No. 2

#	Name	Serving			Passing			Serving			Passing		
5	Chilsom	2	13	0	2	213	1	21	2	3		233	
3	Clark	1	22		1		22		32	4	33		2
2	Hammer	2	21	3	1211	2			22	3	2111		

the head coach know about this weak passing. In game No. 2, Hammer's third "1" pass should trigger the statistician to notify the head coach immediately.

Computing Options
Serving Efficiency

This statistic gives an overall point value rating for all of the serves performed by either a team or an individual. Because it takes into consideration the ability of both the server and the passer, it is the best indicator for the effectiveness of serving. It goes beyond merely telling how many aces and errors are amassed. Using the rating system already presented, the statistician totals the points and divides the sum by the number of attempts. The resulting figure is commonly called serving efficiency and gives an average rating for all serves of the team or an individual. In order to consider statistical significance, this figure should be rounded to the nearest one-hundredth of a point. An efficiency calculated as 2.135 should be rounded to 2.14 rather than 2.1.

---
computing serving efficiency
sum of serving ratings/number of service attempts = average rating per serve*

*this figure is commonly rounded to tenths (e.g., 2.1) but should be rounded to hundredths (e.g., 2.14)

Some coaches prefer converting this rating to a percentage value. By dividing the average rating per serve by four (possible points), a percentage rating for the serving efficiency can be attained. Players may have an easier time relating to percentage values such as 48 percent rather than to a 1.90 point rating. It is up to the coach to determine which figure to use. Figure 1-5 shows raw data from a match and an example of how these two types of ratings are computed. Efficiency averages for the three players, Chilsom, Clark and Hammer, have been calculated. Chilsom served a total of eight times in two games. A rating of 0 to 4 was given to each serve based on the accuracy of the opponent's pass. The sum of the rating points she received for the eight serves was 14. The serve efficiency for Chilsom is calculated by dividing the 14 points by eight serves = 1.75 serving efficiency or 44 percent. Clark's totals are 14/6 for a 2.33 efficiency or 58 percent. Hammer served seven times and scored 15 points for a 2.14 efficiency or 54 percent. The three players together had 43 points and 21 serve attempts for a 2.05 serving efficiency or 51 percent. The exact calculation for Chilsom's serving efficiency is as follows:

- point value: 14/8 = 1.75
- percentage: 1.75/4 = 0.4375 = 44 percent.

Going a step further, a coach could find out what percentage of the player(s)' serves were scored as 3s, 2s, 1s and aces.

Passing Efficiency

This statistic gives an overall point value rating for all of the initial passing opportunities directly from the serve reception. Passing efficiency is a good indicator of how effective the setter can be in running the offense. Keep in mind that a perfect passing efficiency is 3.0—not 4.0. An overall rating of 3.0 would mean that the setter has optimum opportunities on every pass to set any hitter. Using the rating system already presented, the statistician totals the passing points and divides the sum by the number of passing attempts. The resulting figure is commonly called passing or serve reception efficiency and gives an average rating for all passes of the team or an individual. In order to consider statistical significance, this figure should be rounded to the nearest one-hundredth of a point. An effi-

---
computing serve reception efficiency
sum of reception ratings/number of attempts = average rating per reception*

*this figure is commonly rounded to tenths (e.g., 2.3), but should be rounded to hundredths (e.g., 2.34)
---

ciency calculated as 2.335 should be rounded to 2.34 rather than 2.3.

To convert the point value to a percentage value, traditionally, the point value has been divided by four (possible points), similar to the way the serving efficiency percentage computation is done. Since 3.0 is a perfect passing value, the perfect percentage value would then turn out to be 75 percent. This can cause some confusion because normally one would think of a perfect percentage value as 100 percent. If it makes more sense for your team, divide the passing efficiency point value by three (three points is perfect). The result will be that a perfect percentage value would be 100 percent rather than 75 percent. Figure 1-6 shows raw data from a match and an example of how to calculate the average point value and the percentage for passing efficiency using both of the methods described above.

Figure 1-6: Example of Passing Efficiency

Name	Game 1	Game 2	efficiency	pct./4	pct./3	3s	2s	1s	0s
Chilsom	22131	233	17/8=2.13	53	71	38	38	25	0
Clark	122	332	13/6=2.17	54	72	33	5	17	0
Hammer	12112	2111	12/9=1.33	33	44	0	33	67	0
Totals	21/13=1.62	21/10=2.10	42/23=1.83	46	61	22	39	39	0

In the example, Chilsom had eight opportunities to pass served balls and was awarded 17 rating points for those eight passes, giving a passing efficiency for this game of 17/8, which equals a 2.13 efficiency. Chilsom's passing percentage is 53 percent (dividing by four) or 71 percent (dividing by three). Clark passed six balls which totaled 13 rating points, equaling a 2.17 passing efficiency. Clark's passing percentage is either 54 percent or 72 percent. Many coaches also go a bit

Figure 1-5: Example of Serving Efficiency

Name	Game 1	Game 2	Serving efficiency	Serving pct.	3s	2s	1s	4s	0s
Chilsom	2130	2123	14/8=1.75	44	25	38	25	0	13
Clark	122	324	14/6=2.33	58	16	50	16	16	0
Hammer	2213	223	15/7=2.14	54	29	57	14	0	0
Totals	19/11=1.73	24/10=2.40	43/21=2.05	51	24	48	19	5	5

further and calculate what percentage of the passes were scored as 3s, 2s and 1s. The exact calculation for the average of Chilsom's, Clark's and Hammer's passing is as follows:
•point value:
$(17+13+12)/(8+6+9) = 42/23 = 1.826 = 1.83$
•percentage using four points as the divider:
$1.826/4 = 0.456 = 46$ percent
•percentage using three points as the divider:
$1.826/3 = 0.608 = 61$ percent

Ace-To-Error Ratio

This statistic compares the number of service aces to the number of service errors. In combination with the serving efficiency, this statistic can assist the coach in evaluating the effectiveness of the serving philosophy. For example, a coach with an aggressive serving philosophy will want players to serve the ball "tougher" and will expect more errors. These tough serves are meant to put pressure on the passers, resulting in lower passing efficiencies for the opponents. A less aggressive serving philosophy usually results in fewer errors, but the opponents may have higher passing efficiencies, which should enhance their offense. A more thorough discussion of these comparisons is found later in the section on interpreting the data.

computing ace-to-error ratio
total number of aces/number of errors = ace-to-error ratio (A/E)

Figure 1-7 shows examples of how to calculate ace-to-error ratios. All of the information needed to calculate the ratio can be found on a normal serving chart. Simply count the number of 4s for aces and the number of 0s for errors. As shown in Figure 1-7, Terrel had a total of three aces and two errors in the three games. The ace-to-error ratio of 1.5 is arrived at

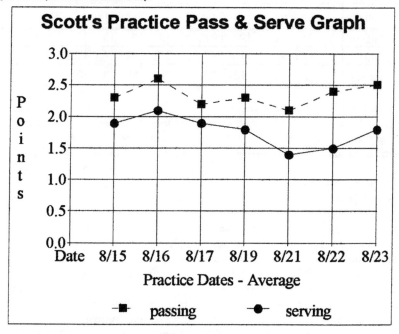

Figure 1-8: Sample Practice Pass and Serve Graph

which calculates to an ace-to-error ratio of 1.0. As a group, the three players had seven aces and eight errors, making their combined ace-to-error ratio .88. (It is possible to have an ace-to-error ratio of 0 if the player has no aces and one or more errors.)

Reporting Options
Practice Pass and Serve Graph - Appendix, Form 3

This graph can be helpful in giving team members a more visual idea of the practice performance. A graph for each player can be posted and updated after each practice session. Use the data recorded on the Practice Pass and Serve Chart to compute the passing and serving efficiencies each day. Players can measure their own progress and set daily goals. Coaches also get a good visual image of a player's consistency in practice and other specific information, which can be helpful in planning practices. Figure 1-8 shows an abbreviated graph for one player, Scott, covering only a few days of practice. An expanded form is found in the Appendix (Form 3). It is easy to see

trends in an individual player's performance with this tool.

Summary Charts and Graphs
Individual Pass and Serve Chart - Appendix, Form 4

This chart gives a match-by-match summary of an individual player's passing and serving. It is always helpful to follow a player's performance throughout the season and compare individual performance with team performance. It is up to the coach whether or not to post this type of chart. Some coaches prefer to keep statistics for coaching purposes only. Other coaches use statistical information during individual conferences where the player's performance and goals are discussed. Once again, this information can serve as a motivating factor or a reality check for many athletes who question decisions coaches make about playing time. Many sport psychologists believe that it is important for players to receive this type of objective feedback.

Figure 1-9 shows an abbreviated individual pass and serve chart. A manager can compile all of the data for this chart by consulting the Match Pass and Serve Statistics chart. The date of the match, opponent, site and won/lost results are entered in chronological order. Prior to each match, the player will set passing and serving goals for the upcoming match. After the match, the form is completed with the computations from the raw data. In Figure 1-9, the chart shows that on

Figure 1-7: Ace-to-Error Ratio From Serving Chart

Name	Serving Scores			Serving		A/E
	Game 1	Game 2	Game 3	efficiency	pct./4	ratio
Terrel	3244	103	403	24/10=2/4	60	3/2=1.5
Kemp	2210	120	240	14/10=1.4	35	1/3=.33
Robertson	4401	340	30	19/9=2.11	53	3/3=1.0
Totals	27/12=2.25	14/9=1.56	16/8=2/0	57/29=1.97	49	7/8=.88

by dividing three aces by two errors. Terrel's serving efficiency, calculated from the raw data in the three games, is 2.40 or 60 percent. Kemp had one ace and three errors in three games, which calculates to an ace-to-error ratio of .33. Robertson had three aces and three errors,

Figure 1-9: Sample Individual Pass and Serve Chart

Name: Johnson				Passing				Serving				
Date	Opponent	W/L	Site	Goal	Actual	% Perfect	ER	Goal	Actual	Aces	ER	A/E
9/2	FSU	W	home	2.1	2.21	41%	1	1.8	1.72	0	1	0
9/4	USC	W	Columbia	2.1	2.13	48%	0	1.8	1.64	0	2	0
9/9	UM	L	home	2.2	2.01	39%	2	1.8	1.68	1	2	0.5

Sept. 9, the team lost to UM. Johnson's goals for the match were to pass at an efficiency of 2.2 and serve at an efficiency of 1.8. He actually passed 39 percent of the passes perfectly (3s) and averaged a 2.01 efficiency with two reception errors. The serving totals averaged an efficiency of 1.68–one service ace and two service er-

Figure 1-10: Abbreviated Season Pass and Serve Chart

Team Chart				Passing				Serving				
Date	Opponent	W/L	Site	Goal	Actual	% Perfect	ER	Goal	Actual	Aces	ER	A/E
9/2	FSU	W	home	2.2	2.33	42%	2	1.9	1.84	2	4	0.5
9/4	USC	W	Columbia	2.2	2.41	51%	1	1.9	1.75	5	8	0.63
9/9	UM	L	home	2.3	2.16	39%	4	1.9	1.61	2	7	0.29

rors. The ace-to-error ratio of 0.5 is arrived at by dividing one ace by two errors.

Season Pass and Serve Chart - Appendix, Form 5

This tool provides a vehicle for displaying team match averages, which can be posted in the team lockerroom. As the season advances, it will be easy to see tendencies. Having hard data helps players set realistic team performance goals. Space is available on this form to list goals in each area. If individual passing and serving data is shared with players, this chart can help them to see how their averages compare to team averages.

Figure 1-10 shows an abbreviated season pass and serve chart. It is completed much like the individual chart. The team or coach should set performance goals for passing and serving before the match. Following the match, the manager can complete the form with team totals from the match.

Season Pass and Serve Graph - Appendix, Form 6

This graph can display the same information as the Season Pass and Serve Chart. Most players find it easier to get an overall picture of data when it is presented in a more visual manner, so this graphic form might be more effective than traditional charts. Colored pens can be used to contrast passing and serving data. Write the opponents on the vertical lines

at the bottom of the graph. Plot your team's match averages on the vertical line corresponding to the opponent. Indicate wins and losses below the opponent's names. It is easy with this type of presentation to see a correlation between passing and serving efficiencies and win/loss results.

Figure 1-11 shows an example of team passing and serving over a period of nine matches during the season. The graph shows trends during the season, indicating slumps and highlights. Comparing these values with wins and losses may give the coach information about minimal values needed to be successful. Posting a graph like this in the lockerroom may also give your team a reality check about its performance from match to match! For even more individual information, one can plot an individual player's pass and serve averages to see how one

player has done in comparison with the team averages. In Figure 1-11, the coach could easily point out to Beck that his passing is generally above the team averages, but his serving is below team averages. His focus in practice should be serving.

Data Interpretation
Match Pass and Serve Statistics

The sample pass and serve chart, Figures 1-12 a and b (pages 6 and 7), shows the raw data from the games and the totals which were calculated following the match. During the match, the coach can use this information to make adjustments and personnel changes. Players will often show varying levels of performance from match to match. For example, when a normally good passer is having a bad night, it is important for the coach to make adjustments during the match to try to improve the overall performance of the team. Some coaches choose not to make an adjustment in the passing, possibly because they feel there are no better options. If this is the case, the coach will at least know why the team is struggling. An examination of this sample chart reveals the following tendencies, strengths and weak-

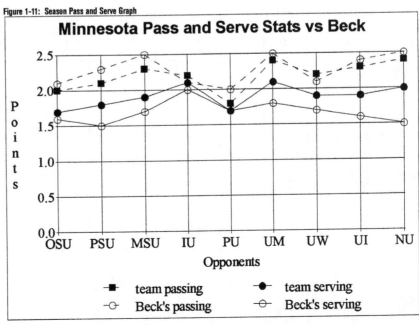

Figure 1-11: Season Pass and Serve Graph

Minnesota Pass and Serve Stats vs Beck

Points vs Opponents (OSU, PSU, MSU, IU, PU, UM, UW, UI, NU)

- ■— team passing
- ●— team serving
- ○— Beck's passing
- ○— Beck's serving

MATCH PASS AND SERVE STATISTICS

SOUTH VS NORTH **DATE: 10/5**

GAME SCORES: 9-15, 15-12, 10-15, 15-9, 15-9 (SOUTH 3-2)

SOUTH: 1 2 3 4 5 6 7 8 9 10 11 12 13 14 15 16 17
OPPONENTS: 1 2 3 4 5 6 7 8 9 10 11 12 13 14 15 16 17

PLAYER # SUBS	GAME 1 SERVING	GAME 1 PASSING	GAME 2 SERVING	GAME 2 PASSING	GAME 3 SERVING	GAME 3 PASSING
CHRIS #1 (X) 2 3	23 2 103	10121	323 24		3 203 1	
HEIDI #2 (X) 2 3	32 214 2	20 0 11	22 332		3 33 3	3
SUE #3 (X) 2 3	1 2112		1112 12		22112	
JENNIFER #4 1 2 3						
EMILY #5 (X) 2 3	2 312	33 2	33 14	32	412	33
BARB #6 1 2 3						
GRETCHEN #7 (X) 2 3	2 312	221 2	30 412	1322 22322	0 321	2 2213 22213
JANE #8 (1) 2 3				12221		22122
JEAN #9 (X) 2 3	44 4	2 3 33	440 333	333	444 303	233
DIANE #10 1 2 3						
1 2 3						
1 2 3						

	GAME 1 SERVING	GAME 1 PASSING	GAME 2 SERVING	GAME 2 PASSING	GAME 3 SERVING	GAME 3 PASSING
TIMEOUTS	1	2	1	2	1	2
SUBSTITUTIONS	1 2 3 4 5 6 7 8 9 10 11 12	1 2 3 4 5 6 7 8 9 10 11 12	1 2 3 4 5 6 7	8 9 10 11 12	1 2 3 4 5 6 7	8 9 10 11 12
TEAM TOTALS	13/6 19/7 28/15	10/5 8/5 17/11	15/7 35/13 13/8	14/5 8/4 19/10	6/3 36/14 18/10	10/4 8/4 25/12
PER GAME	60/28=2.1	35/21 = 1.7	63/28=2.3	41/19=2.2	60/27=2.2	43/20=2.2

MATCH TOTALS

SOUTH VS NORTH

Match Totals (right section)

PLAYER / #SUBS	SERVING ACE/ER RATIO	SERVING EFF.	PASSING EFF.	PASSING PERCENT PERFECT
CHRIS #1 *X*3	1/3=.3	50/23=2.2	7/6=1.2	0/6=0%
HEIDI #2 *X*3	1/2=.5	47/21=2.2	4/5=.8	0/5=0%
SUE #3 *2 3	0/0	24/17=1.4		
JENNIFER #4 *X*3				
EMILY #5 *2 3	2/1=2.0	37/17=2.2	62/23=2.7	17/23=.70
BARB #6 1 2 3				
GRETCHEN #7 *2 3	1/2=.5	33/18=1.8	73/38=1.9	5/38=.10
JANE #8 *2 3			5/2=2.5	1/2=.50
JEAN #9 *2 3	12/9=1.3	69/28=2.5	55/20=2.8	15/20=.80
DIANE #10 *2 3	0/0	11/4=2.8		
1 2 3				
1 2 3				
TOTALS	17/17=1.0	270/124 =2.2	206/94 =2.2	38/94
	3.4 a/g	2.2	2.2	40%

Game 4 / Game 5 (left section)

Rotation markers: 1 2 3 4 5 6 7 8 9 10 11 12 13 14 15 16 17

PLAYER	GAME 4 SERVING	GAME 4 PASSING	GAME 5 SERVING	GAME 5 PASSING
CHRIS #1	322		3221	2
HEIDI #2	0	23	22	
SUE #3	1			
JENNIFER #4				
EMILY #5	2 301	3332 3332 33	32	3231 33
BARB #6				
GRETCHEN #7	0	2231	22	2
JANE #8		23		
JEAN #9	40 3344	3323 32	0 43303	3323
DIANE #10	323		3	

Bottom totals

	GAME 4	GAME 5
TIMEOUTS	1 2	1 2
SUBSTITUTIONS (1-12)	24/14 24/9 11/4 22/8 24/10	24/12 13/5 9/4 2/1 19/7
TEAM TOTALS	2/1 50/24=2.1 (serving) 57/22 = 2.6 (passing)	0/0 37/17=2.1 (serving) 30/12 = 2.5 (passing)
PER GAME		

nesses during this match:

• The chart shows which players are passing poorly, indicating a need to adjust the serve reception formation or substitute the players. Specifically, in game No. 1, Schaefer and Olhausen did not pass well. Statistics in game Nos. 2 through 5 indicate that an adjustment was made so that they did not pass the serve (they had only one passing attempt in four games), but still remained in the line-up and served. Note that the team passed at an efficiency of only 1.67 in game No. 1. The team improved to 2.16 in game No. 2, when Schaefer and Olhausen were taken out of the serve reception pattern.

• The coaching staff should ask the person recording the passing and serving statistics to inform them if a particular player is having problems in one area. For example, it would be wise for the statistician to tell the coach about Olhausen's passing problems in game No. 1.

• The chart shows which players are serving effectively and which are not and can indicate a need to make adjustments in the line-up or a need to change the serving strategy. For example, in game Nos. 1 and 2, Schintz scored five aces and had only one error using her jump serve. She was a "hot" server and the coach certainly wanted her to continue using her jump serve. (Coaches should design some way to note which serve attempts are jump serves—perhaps a slash through the attempt.) Jackson, however, served 11 times for a total of 15 points (15/11=1.36)—not an impressive efficiency. Jackson did not make any errors, but her serve was either weak or she was constantly serving to a very good passer. These situations were important factors as the match progressed.

• The number of passing attempts for specific players most likely indicates the serving strategy of the opponents. Although Ahlquist is a primary passer and one of this team's best, she has few attempts. After game No. 1, Dahl is getting nearly every serve. Although she is not passing every serve poorly, she is not consistent enough to allow the team's offense to be effective against an opponent with a very strong block. Passing statistics from game Nos. 4 and 5 show how much the passing efficiency improved when Dahl was taken out of the serve reception pattern, making it possible for Ahlquist and Schintz to pass almost all of the serves. Team passing efficiency for game Nos. 4

and 5 improved to 2.59 and 2.50, respectively. This one adjustment by the coach was probably a significant factor in the team's success in the last two games.

• In the fourth game, Schintz remains a "hot" server and Ahlquist is passing well. These facts are important considerations as the coach determines the line-up and service order for the fifth game of the match. If rally scoring is used in the fifth game, the coach should pay particular attention to selecting good match-ups and a strong service order. Season averages can be useful for making these determinations, but the coach should also carefully consider the statistics from the current match. If certain players are having the matches of their lives, take advantage of it!

• The individual match totals show some obvious strengths and weaknesses. Schintz had an outstanding match. She had an ace-to-error serving ratio of 1.3; a serving efficiency of 2.5; a passing efficiency of 2.8; and 80 percent of her passes were "perfect" 3s. Jackson (the setter) needs to work on serving more effectively, because she had a serving efficiency of only 1.41 for the match. Jackson should definitely not be one of the first servers for the team. Schaefer (1.17 passing efficiency), Olhausen (0.8 passing efficiency) and Dahl (1.92 passing efficiency) need to improve their passing efficiencies before they can be primary passers in the team line-up. Comparisons with season averages will tell the coach if these statistics follow the player(s) previous trends or if the player(s) had a particularly good or bad night.

The match totals are calculated at the conclusion of the match and can be found at the bottom of the sample form. For this match the team had an ace-to-error ratio of 1.0; a serving efficiency of 2.18; a passing efficiency of 2.19; and passed 40 percent of the opponent's serves perfectly. The per-game averages show the averages from this match. If the coach wanted more data, it is possible to determine the team's average number of serves and passing attempts in each game. To arrive at these figures, divide the raw score totals in each category by the number of games played in the match. For this match, the team averaged 3.4 aces per game (17 aces/5 games = 3.4) and 3.4 service errors per game (17 errors/5 games = 3.4). Following the same procedure, the per-game statistics could also show the coach the av-

erage number of serving attempts per game (124 attempts/5 games = 24.8) and the average number of passing attempts per game (94 attempts /5 games = 18.8). As the season progresses, these averages are helpful in planning (e.g., substitution patterns).

Ace-to-Error Ratio

Usually, a coach wants players to have more aces than errors–and will say so! However, the coach's serving philosophy will delineate exactly what ace-to-error ratio is acceptable. A coach with an aggressive serving philosophy–using jump serves and tough floaters–will more than likely have to settle for a higher error rate. Conversely, a coach who wants the ball put safely into play and is depending on the team's ability to block and play defense will be less accepting of service errors.

At some point, a coach must weigh how effective it is to have a serving strategy which "just puts the ball in play." (Translation: "Do not miss your serve!") For higher levels of play, a "lollipop" serve is the equivalent of giving an immediate side-out to the opponents, as such a serve usually results in a perfect pass. There is nothing more difficult to defend against than a good setter with a number of options and hitters with this kind of advantage. The key to good coaching is to pick the most effective serving strategy for your team. If your players are easily scoring points, there is no need to risk "tougher" serves. But if the opponents are routinely siding out on your serve, the coach may want to consider taking more risks by using a tougher serve. Tough serves are not always "hard" ones—a well-placed short serve can be very tough. The serving strategy may change from match to match based on the strengths and weaknesses of the opponents—it may even change rotation by rotation during a game. For example, if you are facing a team with an exceptionally strong middle attacker, it is a good strategy to serve aggressively when that player is in the front row. Hopefully, an aggressive serve will result in a less-than-perfect pass and take the middle hitting option away from the setter. In combination with serving efficiency, the ace-to-error ratio will give the coach some information about how aggressively the team can afford to serve. Another guideline for the coach to use in determining acceptable ace-to-error ratios is that your ace-to-error ratio should be comparable to the points per rotation ratio (to be discussed in Chapter 4).

Using All of Your Serve and Serve Reception Data

•Situation 1: Kirchner is a high school player who plays on a good team in an above average conference. She uses an aggressive jump serve and scores a lot of points, but also has a lot of errors. At mid-season she has accumulated 35 aces, but has also committed 58 errors. Dividing 35 aces by 58 errors will give an ace-to-error ratio of 0.6. This translates to approximately six aces for every 10 errors. For an aggressive jump server, this ace-to-error ratio may be an acceptable one, depending upon your team's level of play. The coach needs to consider if this aggressive tactic is productive and fits into the overall serving strategy. Checking Kirchner's serve efficiency statistic, her individual points per rotation value (see Chapter 4 on points per rotation) and the team points per rotation ratio may give good, definitive information for the coach's decision. Her serve efficiency rating is 2.1 and her points per rotation ratio is 0.9. The team points per rotation ratio (PPR) is 1.3. Roughly, this means that the team is scoring an average of 1.3 points each time someone rotates back to take her term of service. Kirchner's PPR is lower than the team average, which might indicate to the coach that the team is suffering when she serves because she is missing too many serves (point scoring opportunities). However, Kirchner's serving efficiency of 2.1 is relatively high, indicating that the opponents may have trouble passing her serve. In the end, the coach may decide that she is giving the team an additional dimension and it is an acceptable risk, as long as the other players serve more consistently.

•Situation 2: Danielson is an "AAA" open player. He uses a float serve, which is delivered with good velocity. He has scored 29 aces and committed 26 errors. In trying to determine if Danielson's serve is effective and efficient, the coach can calculate his ace-to-error ratio by dividing his aces by the number of errors (29/26 = 1.1) This ace-to-error ratio is slightly better than one ace for every error. Generally, an ace-to-error ratio of 1.0 or higher is considered good for a person who uses a "tough" float serve. Danielson's serving efficiency is 1.9 so far this season and his points per rotation ratio is 0.7. His team's points per rotation ratio is 0.5 and the team serving efficiency is 1.6. The combination of his high efficiency rating, ace-to-error ratio (higher than the team average) and points per rotation ratio (also higher than the team average) shows that Danielson's statistics make him a very strong, effective server—probably the best on his team.

•Situation 3: The coach of a collegiate team has a player, Schintz, who is a very erratic jump server. Many times after Schintz has missed several jump serves during a match, the coach tells her to "stay down" and use a float serve rather than her jump serve. Her float serve is not very strong and often turns out to be a "lollipop." The coach is trying to determine what serving strategy (other than to have her practice and become better and more consistent) to use during a match—should she go for the more aggressive jump serve or take her chances with the lollipop? The coach should consider many statistics and individual situations in making this decision about serving strategy. Some of them are:

▲Is the team not scoring because the opponents are passing exceptionally well and siding out on every serve? If so, more aggressive serving is needed and the coach may as well have Schintz jump serve instead of serving a "lollipop."

▲Is the team not scoring because of missed serves rather than the opponent's perfect passing and side-outs? If so, maybe it is better to have Schintz serve a "lollipop" in hopes that your team can block and/or dig the opponent's attacks and score in transition. Assuming the rest of the team is serving well and scoring points, it may be worth the risk to have Schintz use her jump serve. However, if Schintz is serving when one of your strongest scoring rotations is at the net, you may want to change your rotation order so that she is serving with a weaker scoring rotation.

▲Is Schintz a pressure player? Does she rise to the occasion in a tight situation or does she make more errors? Some players are every effective with a jump serve when there is no pressure and others do better in a pressure-packed situation. It would be important to know Schintz's tendencies. If she responds well to pressure, it might be worth the risk to have her jump serve with the score at 13-13, even if she has missed several serves earlier in the game.

▲Charting a player's tendencies in all game situations, knowing all of your players' serving efficiencies and ratios and considering the specific game situation will be important in making the best decisions about serving strategy.

•Situation 4: The chart in Figure 1-13 shows actual serving data from the University of Minnesota during a four-year period. In year No. 1, several players were learning the jump serve but were not permitted to use it during competitive matches due to inconsistency. During year No. 2, all three players started using the jump serve in competitive matches. Oesterling used the jump serve exclusively, while Gonzalez and Schaefer used it for at least 90 percent of their service attempts. (Gonzalez graduated in year No. 3, so no statistics were available for

Figure 1-13: Ace-to-Error Ratio Comparison During a Four-Year Period

Player	service aces				service errors				ace-to-error ratio				aces/game			
	1	2	3	4	1	2	3	4	1	2	3	4	1	2	3	4
Oesterling	35	106	60	113	33	83	76	96	1.06	1.28	0.78	1.18	0.31	0.8	0.5	0.77
Gonzalez	48	68	91	na	72	108	122	na	0.67	0.63	0.75	na	0.4	0.55	0.75	na
Schaefer	13	56	66	66	22	111	97	83	0.59	0.51	0.68	0.8	0.15	0.47	0.55	0.5
Team	227	380	326	404	311	565	508	515	0.73	0.67	0.64	0.78	1.86	2.86	2.69	2.68

Year 1 - float serve used exclusively; years 2-4 - jump serve used by these players.

her in year No. 4.) From the data in Figure 1-13, it is easy to see the large increase in service aces and aces per game for all three players if year No. 1 is compared with year Nos. 2-4. Equally obvious is the large increase in service errors. In year Nos. 2-4, the University of Minnesota led the Big Ten Conference in total individual player aces, individual player aces per game, total team aces and team aces per game. These are impressive accomplishments, but without the benefit of ace-to-error ratios, it would be difficult for a coach to determine whether the aces were worth the risk, considering the large number of errors. Remember, an ace-to-error ratio of .60 is usually considered good for a jump server who serves the ball with good velocity. The coach of this team used the following rationale for proceeding with the strategy of having Oesterling, Gonzalez and Schaefer use a jump serve:

▲Minnesota had good passing off serve reception and was very good at siding out—missed serves did not present a huge problem.

▲Minnesota had weak blocking and back-court defense, making it difficult to score points when serving—so why not serve tougher, challenging the opponent's passers and hopefully scoring more points off the serve?

▲Many of the teams in the Big Ten had very strong middle attacks—a tougher serve made it more difficult for them to get a perfect pass where they could run the middle attack at will (a poor pass usually gives the blocking team an advantage because the set is more predictable).

▲The jump serve gave Minnesota a mental edge in competition—the team seemed to be more aggressive when it used this tactic and the opponents seemed to be overly focused on dealing with this tactic.

▲Even though Schaefer bordered on marginal with an ace-to-error ratio near or below .60, she became more focused as the games went on and was often at her best at the end of a game in high pressure situations.

▲Oesterling was more consistent with her jump serve than her float serve. Gonzalez had a good float serve she could use if necessary, but her jumper was deadly. Schaefer had a weak float serve commonly referred to as a "lollipop."

What Are Good Passing and Serving Statistics?

Coaches will want to set specific team and individual passing and serving goals. The goal setting process will not only take into account your own players' skills, it should also take into consideration the skills of your opponents. For example, if the teams you play have some exceptional servers–especially jump servers–you may adjust your team passing efficiency goal to a slightly lower level. Conversely, if the opponents are not aggressive servers, you may set your passing efficiency goals higher than usual. Passing is usually better at higher levels of play. Typically, at higher levels of play, teams will score fewer service aces and suffer fewer reception errors.

Jim Coleman has provided statistical ranges for various levels of play. The following ranges reflect normal values achieved for passing and serving during

Normal Passing and Serving Statistics			
Serve Receive (Passing)		Serving	
High School/"B" Open	1.8-1.9	High School/"B" Open	2.1-2.2
Collegiate/"AA" Open	2.1-2.2	Collegiate/"AA" Open	1.8-1.9
"AAA" Open	2.2-2.3	"AAA" Open	1.7-1.8
International	2.4-2.5	International	1.5-1.6

competition. Teams at the top levels of each category may perform significantly better. The "Open" play categories are reflective of standardized adult levels of competition for USA Volleyball. At higher levels of play, outstanding individual servers will average anywhere from .6 to .9 aces per game.

Notice the correlation between serve and serve reception statistics. Teams which are more highly skilled have better passing, resulting in lower serve efficiencies for the opponents.

Summary

•**Serve efficiency** statistics give an overall rating of serves based on how the opponents pass each serve. This is probably the single best indicator of an individual player's effectiveness in serving because it is dependent upon both the skill of the server and the opponent's passing ability. Statistics which only give the coach information about whether the "player misses or makes" the serve are not very helpful in evaluating the overall strategies of the team.

•**Passing efficiency** gives an overall rating of how accurately the individual player passes each serve to the desired "target" area on the court. The efficiency rating gives the coach a method for evaluating whether the team's passing ability will allow the setter to run the team offense effectively. The individual player's passing efficiency will also give the coach information to use in selecting the team's best passers objectively and ultimately will help the coach to design the most efficient team serve reception formations.

•**Ace-to-error ratio** compares the number of service aces to the number of service errors. A key to good coaching is to develop a serving philosophy based upon the strengths and weaknesses of the team. Usually, if your team is easily scoring points, there is no need to risk tougher serves. However, if the opponents are easily siding out, preventing your team from scoring points, the coach may need to consider taking more risks with tougher serves. It is important for the coach to determine specifically why the team may be having scoring problems.

•**Pass and serve statistics** taken during the match give the coach valuable information for making adjustments in personnel and strategy as the match progresses. These same statistics compiled as per game averages throughout the season can produce trends in team and individual performance which will be critical to the technical and tactical decisions the coach makes about the team.

Chapter 2

Hitting, Blocking, Assists and Digs

As the sport of volleyball has developed, the game strategy has become more and more sophisticated. The tactics surrounding hitting and blocking have improved most dramatically. To the fan in the stands, the play at the net is probably the most exciting part of this fast-paced game. Men's volleyball is now primarily won or lost at the net (hitting and blocking). While back-court defense is more important in the women's game, the dominant teams still rely on strong play at the net to be successful consistently. Japan once dominated the women's game because of its ball control and ability to dig almost every ball, but as other teams refined their offensive systems, it has become more difficult to dominate the game with back-court skills. Coaches now generally agree that it is possible to win with outstanding back-court defensive play, but a team with the most dominant net play will usually be more successful. One only needs to watch the elite teams and recent Olympic competition to realize how important these components have become. Therefore, it is imperative for coaches to analyze the effectiveness of net play by evaluating hitting and blocking statistics. These statistics can be analyzed both during play and after a match. Additionally, it is important for volleyball to help provide statistics for the media to use to publicize the sport. The media does not usually understand many of the statistics used in volleyball, but sportswriters can easily see and understand hitting and blocking (e.g., kills and stuff blocks). As advocates for the sport, coaches have an obligation to provide the media with information and statistics that are easy to use and will enhance the exposure given to volleyball.

The continued sophistication of offensive strategy is often determined extensively by the improvement in the skill level of setters. It is difficult to run any type of potent offensive system without a setter who understands the nuances of the game. In order for the hitters to be successful, the setter must deliver a good set into an area where the hitter has a chance to be effective. Assists are used to track the effectiveness of the setters. An assist is awarded to the setter when a ball is directed to the hitter, who scores a kill. Obviously, the ability of the setter to gain an assist is directly related to the team's passing skills and the ability of the hitters to "put the ball away" or score a kill. For this reason, assists have become more of a media statistic for setters rather than a true evaluation of the setter's ability. Another factor affecting the number of assists scored by setters is the length of the games played—setters score more assists in games that last longer. A very good team that wins most of its matches in three short games may have considerably fewer assists. However, in general, the nation's leading setters usually come with higher assist averages and play for teams with a powerful offense.

Following is a detailed explanation of the most commonly accepted methods of gathering and computing statistics for hitting, blocking, assists and digs. This chapter will prepare the reader to understand how these statistics are recorded, calculated and correlated. Many different charts are presented and it is the coach's decision to select the statistics and charts that will meet the needs of a particular team. With the knowledge presented in the first two chapters it will be possible, then, to complete an Official Volleyball Box Score, found in Chapter 3. (For further reference, the *National Volleyball Statistics Manual* is an excellent resource for more detailed explanations. The definitions used in this chapter come from the AVCA manual.) Other rating systems and recording options are presented in Chapters 5 and 7 on charting and in Chapter 8, which deals with computerized statistics programs.

The Rating System
The Attack

An attack attempt is charged to a player any time the player attempts to hit the ball over the net into the opponent's court. The ball may be spiked, set, tipped or hit as an overhead contact. An overpass or a free ball pass should not be considered an attack attempt. There are three possible classifications for an attack attempt:

•**Kill (K)** - Any attempt which is not returnable by the opponent or any attack attempt which leads directly to a blocking error by the opponent. A kill leads directly to a point or side-out. A player who is awarded a kill also receives an attack attempt.

•**Attack Error (E)** - An attack error is charged to a player whenever an attack or attacker:

a. hits the ball out-of-bounds;
b. hits the ball into the net and is called for a "four hits" violation;
c. is blocked down by the opponent on the same side and the ball cannot be kept in play by the attacker's team;
d. goes into the net;
e. is called for a center line violation;
f. is called for an illegal contact on the attack; or
g. hits the ball into the net antenna.

•**0 Attack (ATT)** - Any attack attempt which is kept in play by the opponent. This is usually recorded on the statistical sheet with a "0". The sum of all hitting attempts is called Total Attempts (TA). To get this sum, add all kills, errors and 0 attempts: **kills + errors + 0 attacks = total attempts.**

This rating system for attacks is used virtually universally. All levels of play, including the U.S. national teams, classify attacks with the above system. Some computer programs and coaches further separate kills as those scored in transition and those scored directly from serve reception. These concepts will be discussed at length later in this chapter and in

The Block

The system used for rating the act of blocking on the Official Box Score is the most common system used in volleyball. In this rating system, to be credited statistically with a block (sometimes referred to as a "stuff") the player or players must block the ball back into the opponent's court, leading directly to a point or side-out. An attack which is touched by the blocker(s) but remains in play does not count as a block in the Official Box Score. Blocks are rated as one of the following:

•**A block solo (BS)** is awarded to a player whenever that player blocks the ball into the opponent's court leading directly to a point or side-out. That player is the only one attempting to block the ball. If the blocked ball falls or is deflected back on the opponent's side and is played by an opponent who does not have a legitimate chance to keep the ball in play, then the blocker is still awarded a block solo.

•**A block assist (BA)** is awarded whenever two or three players block the ball into the opponent's court for a point or a side-out. Each player receives a block assist even though only one player actually blocks the ball. Two players may get block assists even if they are separated by 3 to 4 feet along the net and only one player blocks the ball. If the opinion of the statistician is that the players were working in tandem to block an area of the net, then each receives an assist.

•**A block error (BE)** occurs whenever an official calls a blocker for a violation. A ball that is deflected off the blocker and lands out-of-bounds on the blocker's side of the net is considered a kill for the attacker, not an error for the blocker (no tally is given to the blocker). Common blocking errors are:

   a. blocker goes into the net;
   b. blocker is called for a center line violation;
   c. a back-row player is called for blocking the ball; or
   d. blocker is called for reaching over the net (e.g., blocking a set).

Some more advanced rating systems further separate blocking actions as stuff blocks and control blocks—especially computer-generated statistics. (The U.S. national teams use this system.) A stuff block is any block which ends play, leading directly to a point or side-out. Essen-

tially, a control block is an attack that is partially blocked and remains in play on the blocker's side of the net. It is slowed down or funneled to the back-court defense and is then controlled by the defense for a transition attack. Additional discussion about this type of control block is found in Chapter 8, Computerized Statistics Software. (A more complete description of situations and rules for counting blocks for the Official Box Score can be found in the *National Volleyball Statistics Manual.*)

Assists

The assist category is found on the Official Box Score. Currently, most sport governing bodies (NCAA, NAIA, NJCAA, etc.) tabulate setter assists as one of the tools in the evaluation process for recognizing outstanding setters. Some governing bodies also require schools to tabulate the number of setting attempts made by players so that an assist percentage/efficiency can be calculated. However, the Official Box Score does not have a column for reporting assist attempts. There are three possible outcomes of a ball that is being set:

•**An assist (A)** is awarded to any player who passes, sets or digs the ball to a teammate resulting in an attack for a kill. (The guidelines for awarding an assist in volleyball are much the same as those used in awarding an assist in basketball.)

•**An assist error (AE)** or **ball handling error (BHE)** is given to a player for any attempted set resulting in an illegal action called by the official (e.g., double contact, lift).

•**A zero assist (0)** is given to any player who sets a ball that does not directly lead to a kill or a side-out. Documentation of a zero assist on the worksheet is only required if the statistician is calculating assist percentage.

Digs

A dig is awarded whenever a player legally plays a ball that has been attacked by the opposition. Digs are only awarded for receiving an attacked ball that is subsequently kept in play. The ball can be kept in play on the digger's side of the net or the ball can go over the net to the opposition's side. A dump by the setter is considered an attack. Tips or dinks are also considered an attack. A ball played up from a deflection off a block is not

considered an attack and therefore cannot be classified as a dig. Digs (D) are simply recorded by tallies on a statistical form and then totaled at the end of a game and/or match. If the player attempting a dig is called for an illegal play of the ball (e.g., lift or double hit), that player is charged with a ball handling error (BHE).

Recording Options
AVCA Worksheet - Appendix, Form 7

The AVCA Worksheet is used to complete the AVCA Box Score form at the end of the match. It is a tool most often used by a "statistics crew" rather than someone on the team bench. Other types of forms provide the coaches with more definitive information as the match progresses. However, if there is a shortage of people who are available for a statistics crew, the worksheet can be kept on the bench by a manager(s) who might even record statistics for both teams during the match. It is highly desirable for the coach to find three people to serve as a statistics crew. Managers can be used for recording "coaching statistics" from the bench. Coaching statistics refer to forms and/or charts designated by the coach to record tendencies in team play which are valuable as coaching aids during a match. Usually, coaching statistics are neither necessary nor valuable to the media. The information on the AVCA Worksheet comprises the highlights of the match which are used by the media to report the match.

Many different symbols can be used to mark kills, errors and 0 attacks. The easiest way to record attacks is by drawing an open circle every time an attack is made and then using the following symbols (see Appendix, Form 7):

Pick the symbols that are easiest for you. Normally, the bottom section of the worksheet is completed using tallies for every skill recorded (assists, aces, blocks and digs). However, if coaches wish to compute an assist efficiency (percent of sets resulting in kills), then the following symbols should be used rather than tallies:

Using a different colored pen for each

game makes it is easy to differentiate one game from another. In situations where coaches do not have the luxury of a statistics crew to cover both teams, each team can keep its own statistics and exchange copies after the match. Worksheets printed on NCR™ (self-carbon) forms ease the process—statisticians merely exchange one of the carbon copies of their team's statistics after the match. In the past few years, schools have been using computers (laptops and PCs) with specialized programs to enter statistics while the match is in progress. Nearly all sta-

Figure 2-1: Abbreviated AVCA Worksheet

Player	No	Game 1	Game 2	Game 3	Game 4	Game 5	K	E	TA	EFF.
Donnell	11	kkkoe	ook	kooo	oeokook	koooo	8	2	24	0.25
Lushine	8	ooo	oo	okkkk	ekk		6	1	13	0.385
Benning	15	okkoe	oookek	kooee	okokkke	ookooe	10	6	29	0.138

Game Totals	Kills	Errors	Attempts	EFF.	Attack Key:
1	5	2	13	0.231	0 = attack (stays in play)
2	3	1	11	0.182	k = kill
3	6	2	14	0.286	e = error
4	8	3	17	0.294	TA = o + e + k
5	2	1	11	0.091	PCT. = k - e / Attempts

TO DISTINGUISH ONE GAME FROM ANOTHER USE DIFFERENT COLORED PENS										
PLAYER	NO	ASSISTS	SA	SE	RE	DIGS	BS	BA	BE	BHE
Donnell	11	11	11	111	1	111111	1	111		1
Lushine	8	111111	1	1		1111		1111	1	11
Benning	15	1	111	1	11	11111	11	11		

tistics used by the U.S. national teams are taken using computers.

Figure 2-1 shows an abbreviated AVCA Worksheet completed for three players, not an entire team. (The attack key on Form 7 is easier to use than the one used in this form for demonstration purposes.) Ideally, a statistics crew of three people should complete this form. One person would serve as the "caller" by verbalizing the action on the court; the other two people would serve as "recorders," documenting the action on the form. There is one recorder for each team. For example, the caller would say, "FSU No. 11 dig, No. 8 set, No. 15 hit for a kill." Then the recorder for FSU records a dig tally for No. 11, an assist tally for No. 8 and a kill for No. 15. Be sure to record attack attempts under the column for the specific game. Tallies for the other skills are recorded, one after another, in the player's area on the bottom section of the chart. If the attack attempt for No. 15 had remained in play, it would be recorded as an attempt (0) and the caller would continue calling the action for the opponents. The recorder for the opponents records the actions of his/her team as the play-by-play is called. At the end

of each game, the hitting statistics (kills, errors, attempts) can be totaled. Formulas for calculations are discussed in the next section.

Attack Chart - Appendix, Form 8

The Attack Chart is used to record every attack attempt by a player. A line is drawn showing the path of the ball after contact by the hitter. The statistician places a line showing the path of the ball after the contact. The line for the ball's path is drawn between the place on the court where the player initiated the hit and the spot where the attack was either terminated (kill) or played by the opponents. Be sure to be as exact as possible about the spatial orientation for the path of the ball so it accurately reflects the action on the court. The result of each hit is marked using the symbols in the key. The purpose of using several different notations in the key is to attempt to describe as closely as possible the path of the ball and the result of each attempt. Attempts that originate near the 3-meter line represent back-row attacks by the hitter. Balls remaining in play, it is assumed, are dug by the opponent. The

"notes" section of the chart is filled in after the charting session. It is meant to be a brief synopsis of what the chart shows. A quick review of the chart reveals the hitting tendencies of each player. Analysis of the charts will be discussed later in the section about interpreting the data. There is also a method for noting the type of set executed before each attack attempt. (Discussion about types of sets is found in Chapters 5 and 7 on charting.)

An assistant coach on the bench routinely keeps attack charts during a match. Different charts can be kept for each game. If only one chart is used for the match, colored pens can be used to distinguish each game. The head coach should decide whether to chart only his/her team or to chart the hitters on both teams. It is not difficult to chart hitting for both teams since the hitting occurs alternately from one side of the net to the other side. Most coaches choose to have separate court diagrams on the chart to diagram hitting during serve reception vs. hitting in transition. Other coaches choose to have a completely separate chart just for serve reception attacks. (This will be discussed at length in Chapter 5.)

Figure 2-2 shows an abbreviated attack chart for two players with a key describing the markings. There were a total of 11 attempts for No. 11: five were kills, two were errors and four remained in play. One of the attempts that remained in play was also touched by a blocker (indicated by the "-" mark). One of the kills landed out-of-bounds, but it was either touched by the blocker or the digger. Player No. 8 had 16 attack attempts: six kills; four errors; and six attempts which remained in play. One of Player No. 8's attacks which remained in play was also touched by a blocker. Can you complete the notes section with the tendencies of each player?

Figure 2-2: Abbreviated Attack Chart

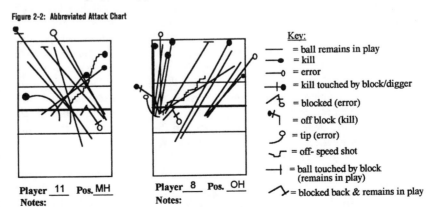

Player __11__ Pos. __MH__
Notes:

Player __8__ Pos. __OH__
Notes:

Key:
— = ball remains in play
—● = kill
—○ = error
—+ = kill touched by block/digger
= blocked (error)
= off block (kill)
= tip (error)
= off- speed shot
—| = ball touched by block (remains in play)
= blocked back & remains in play

Hitting and Blocking Chart -
Appendix, Forms 9 a and b

This chart serves two purposes: First, it allows the statistician to track the hitting of specific players by rotation against the opponent's blockers. Basically, the coach could calculate a hitting efficiency for each player in each rotation. Secondly, it enables the statistician to track the blocking effectiveness of each player by rotation against the opponent's hitters. The Hitting and Blocking Chart should be kept on the bench by a manager or assistant coach during the match. The same person might also be able to keep a similar chart for the opponent's hitting and blocking, giving the head coach a snapshot of the opposition in these two areas. As with other charts, the head coach may wish to give the statistician a list of "triggers" signaling a time when he/she wishes to be notified of certain developing trends. For example, the coach may decide that the statistician should let him/her know when a certain player is or is not scoring on specific shots. Maybe the outside hitter is scoring on shots down the line, but not on cross-court attacks. Or, perhaps the coach says, "Let me know if Tom has more than three hitting errors in rotation No. 1." Another helpful trigger would be for the coach to be alerted when a specific play continually results in a kill (e.g., a wide backset to the right side combined with a shoot set to the middle hitter). The information on this chart and an opponent's chart can be very helpful between games for deciding line-ups and strategy. Separate charts can be used for each game or all games can be kept on the same chart using a different colored pen for each game. Back-row attacks can be charted with a notation of the number of the player who is attacking the ball (see Figure 2-16, page 22).

Figure 2-3 shows an abbreviated hitting and blocking chart for two players. (The complete chart can be found in the Appendix, Forms 9 a and b.) On the complete chart there are three courts for each rotation—a hitting chart for each front-row player in the rotation. The front-row players in the example are No. 10, No. 3 and No. 9. The top circle is used to note the opponent's rotation and front-row players. The bottom circle is for the statistician's team's rotation order. Figure 2-3 shows the opponent's front-row players as No. 2, No. 5 and No. 8. At the beginning of the game, it is helpful to

Figure 2-3: Abbreviated Hitting and Blocking Chart

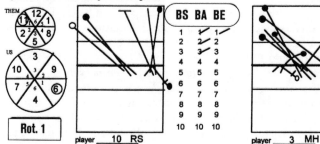

complete the rotation circle (wheel) for each rotation, inserting the line-up for that specific game. The player's numbers are entered in rotation (service order) on the wheel. The small numbers on the inside of the wheel indicate the service order. Player No. 6 is the first server, No. 9 is the second server, No. 3 is the third server, etc. It is customary to circle the setter's number (No. 6 in this example). (A more complete description of rotations is found in Chapter 4.) The statistician charts the attacks using the symbols described in Figure 2-2.

In Figure 2-3, player No. 10 (a right side/opposite) has three kills, one error and a total of seven attempts. Player No. 3 (a middle hitter), has six kills, one error and a total of nine attempts. The blocking for each rotation is tabulated by merely striking through block solos (BS), block assists (BA) or block errors (BE). The blocking represents stuff blocks scored against the opponent's hitters. In Figure 2-3, player No. 3 has totaled two block solos, three block assists and no block errors. Player No. 10 has three block assists, no block solos and one block error.

Set Selection Chart -
Appendix, Forms 10 a and b

The Set Selection Chart is a bit more complicated and allows the coach to gather information about the set selection tendencies of the setter(s) by rotation. It also shows the opponent's rotations so the coach knows which blockers are faced in each rotation. The chart has an area to record the quality of the pass the setter received, the type of set selected, which player receives the set, how good the set was and the result of the attack. Since the sets are kept in chronological order and by rotation, the coach can also note changes in tactics by the setter. Before the game starts, the statistician should complete the rotation wheels with the rotation order for both teams. Each time

the rotation changes, the statistician will move to the proper rotation to record the information about each set. (A detailed description of the types of sets [terminology] is found in Chapter 5.) The statistician must use his/her judgment about the execution of the set (how good was the set placement?). This chart can be kept on the bench by a substitute setter. In situations where it becomes necessary for the coach to insert a substitute setter into the middle of a game, this chart should arm the substitute with good information about specific rotations. It is much better than having a daydreaming setter go into a critical situation!

Figure 2-4 shows an abbreviated set selection chart. The data recorded depicts some of the data chronicled on the Hitting and Blocking Chart in Figure 2-3. The complete notation for the first set is:

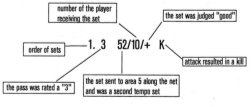

The first set in rotation No. 1 comes after a pass which was rated a "3". Under the set selection area the notation means that the set was a "52" (to area 5 and second tempo—see Chapter 5), the set was made to player No. 10 and it was judged to be a good set based on the location and height. The result of the first set is a kill for the hitter. The fourth set comes after a pass rated a "1" and is delivered as a good (+), high backset (95) to player No. 10. The hitter scores a kill off the blocker's hands (K/B). The fifth set in this rotation comes from a "2" pass. It is a shoot set (31—quick set to area 3), but is judged by the statistician to be a poor set, resulting in a blocked attack and a net error by the hitter. The eighth setting attempt is a ball handling error (BHE) by the setter from a "2" pass.

Figure 2-4: Abbreviated Set Selection Chart

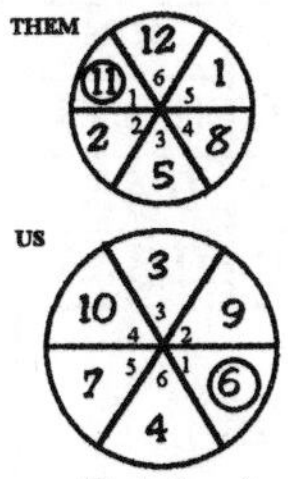

Pass	Set	Result					Notes		
1. 3	52/10/+	K	11.			21.			
2. 2	93/10/o	O	12.			22.			
3. 3	51/3/+	K	13.			23.			
4. 1	95/10/-	K/B	14.			24.			
5. 2	31/3/-	B/NE	15.			25.			
6. 3	51/3/+	O	16.			26.			
7. 2	92/10/o	O	17.			27.			
8. 2	BHE	---	18.			28.			
9. 3	52/10/+	E	19.			29.			
10.			20.			30.			

Key

Pass Ratings:
3 = all options
(perfect pass)

2 = two options-
no middle attack

1 = very limited options

0 = error/RE

Example: 72/3/+

Set Selection:
type/player #/rating

type = area and tempo
(e.g., 31, 52)

rating: + = good
0 = average
- = poor

X (#) = non setter
(player number)

Result:
K = kill
E = error
O = dug
B = blocked/error
BHE = ball handling error

NE = net error
CE = centerline error

Computing Options
Hitting Efficiency

Most experts feel that hitting efficiency is the statistic that correlates most highly with team success. This statistic gives a percentage value, rating the overall effectiveness of the attacks against the opponents. It tells what percentage of the attacks led directly to a point or a side-out and considers attacking errors as part of the equation. Hitting efficiency is sometimes compared to a batting average in baseball. For example, a .300 hitting efficiency in volleyball is considered good, just as a .300 batting average is considered good. However, hitting efficiency and batting averages are not calculated exactly in the same manner. In computing the hitting efficiency for volleyball, the hitter is penalized for hitting errors. To calculate the hitting efficiency, add all of the attack attempts together. The sum is called **Total Attempts (TA).**

Kills + Errors + 0 Attacks = Total Attempts (TA)

computing hitting efficiency
total kills (K) - total errors (E) / total attempts (TA) = hitting efficiency (Eff.)*
*this is also often referred to as hitting percent (Pct.) and/or attack percentage (Att.%)

Hitting efficiency values are routinely reported as percents (%). For example, an efficiency of .250 can also be reported as "hitting 25 percent." It is possible to arrive at a negative hitting efficiency if the number of attack errors exceeds the number of kills. For example, if a player has 12 attack attempts in a game and records three kills and four errors, a negative eight percent hitting efficiency would result. It would be calculated as follows:

(3K - 4 E) / 12 TA = -1 / 12 = -.08 or -8 percent

Figure 2-5 shows an example of some raw hitting data and the conversion to hitting efficiencies using the above formula. All of the information needed to calculate hitting efficiency can be found on a normal worksheet or chart used to record attacks. In Figure 2-5, Donnell had a total of eight kills in five games. She had a total of 24 attack attempts, two of which were hitting errors. Donnell's hitting efficiency or attack percent is calculated as follows:

(8 kills - 2 errors)/24 attack attempts = 6/24 = .250

Lushine had no kills in the first two games, but scored four kills in game No. 3 and two kills in game No. 4. She had only one error in 13 attack attempts. Lushine's hitting efficiency is calculated as follows:

(6 kills - 1 error)/13 attack attempts = 5/13 = .385

Benning played all five games and had a total of 29 attack attempts, with 10 kills and six errors. Benning's hitting efficiency is calculated as follows:

(10 kills - 6 errors)/29 attack attempts = 4/29 = .138

The bottom section of the form provides space for totals of kills, errors, attempts and hitting percentage. This graphic allows the coach to see how the team's attackers performed in each game. All of this information is transferred to the Official Box Score at the end of the match.

Kill Percentage/Efficiency

This statistic gives a value telling what percentage of the attacks result directly in a point or side-out. It does not factor in the number of attack errors. Although it is not often used, it is a valuable source of information for coaches. Basically, this percentage shows the coach which hitters are the most "deadly" or more simply, what percentage of the total attacks result in kills. To compute kill percentage, use the following formula:

computing kill percentage
total kills (K)/total attempts (TA) = kill percentage (K%)

Figure 2-6 (page 18) shows the excerpt of the AVCA Worksheet found in Figure 2-5 with a column added to compare kill percentage and hitting efficiency. Once again, all of the information needed to calculate kill percentage can be found on a normal attack chart or worksheet. In the comparison chart (see Figure 2-6), Donnell had a hitting percent (efficiency) of .250. This can also be calculated as a kill percentage of .333 by dividing her eight kills by 24 attempts. Lushine has a hitting efficiency of .385 and a kill percent of .461 (6/13 = .461). Benning's statistics show the huge difference which can be found between kill percentage and hitting efficiency. Her hitting efficiency is low at .138, but her kill percentage is a much higher .345 value. A large difference in the two values (as in Benning's statistics) usually means that the hitter is

Figure 2-5: Excerpt from AVCA Worksheet - Attack Statistics

Player	No	Game 1	Game 2	Game 3	Game 4	Game 5	K	E	TA	EFF.
Donnell	11	kkkoe	ook	kooo	oeokook	koooo	8	2	24	0.25
Lushine	8	000	oo	okkkk	ekk		6	1	13	0.385
Benning	15	okkoe	ooookek	kooee	okokkke	ookooe	10	6	29	0.138

Game Totals	Kills	Errors	Attempts	EFF.
1	5	2	13	0.231
2	3	1	11	0.182
3	6	2	14	0.286
4	8	3	17	0.294
5	2	1	11	0.091

Attack Key:
0 = attack (stays in play)
k = kill
e = error
TA = o + e + k
PCT. = k - e / Attempts

Figure 2-6: Hitting Efficiency vs. Kill Percentage

Player	No	Game 1	Game 2	Game 3	Game 4	Game 5	K	E	TA	EFF.	K%
Donnell	11	kkkoe	ook	kooo	oeokook	koooo	8	2	24	0.25	0.333
Lushine	8	ooo	oo	okkkk	ekk		6	1	13	0.385	0.461
Benning	15	okkoe	oookek	kooee	okokkke	ookooe	10	6	29	0.138	0.345

Game Totals	Kills	Errors	Attempts	EFF.	Attack Key:
1	5	2	13	0.231	0 = attack (stays in play)
2	3	1	11	0.182	k = kill
3	6	2	14	0.286	e = error
4	8	3	17	0.294	TA = o + e + k
5	2	1	11	0.091	PCT. = k - e / Attempts

getting kills, but with lots of errors. She would probably be described by her coach as "someone with a shot that either hits the opponent's floor, the block or the bleachers!" Benning would probably be a candidate for some "shot-control training" in practice.

Averages in Volleyball

With the exception of hitting and passing efficiencies, most volleyball statistics are commonly reported as "per game" averages rather than as "per match" averages. This is done because the number of games it takes to complete a match can vary from two (in the best two of three) to five (in the best three of five). For this reason, it is obviously important for coaches to have a record of the number of games (not matches) each athlete plays. This information can be found in two places–the Official Score Sheet shows which players participated in a game and the Official Box Score (if used) has a column to record the number of games each athlete played in the match. The rule of thumb is if a player participates in any part of a game, it counts as a game played. There has been a great deal of discussion in coaching circles about using an adjusted formula for computing kills per game in games where "rally scoring" (e.g., speed scoring in the fifth game) is used because these games are much shorter in length. However, at this point, no sports organization has adopted an adjusted formula for use with official volleyball statistics.

Many national organizations compile lists of the top individual and team performances in volleyball and distribute them to the media as the season progresses. The AVCA maintains a comprehensive website whereby weekly statistical information for all divisions is available (www.avca.org). Additionally,

the NCAA prints an annual *Volleyball Records Book*, which lists season leaders and all-time records in almost every category. It includes volleyball information on NCAA women's Division I, II and III; the AVCA maintains a records book for NCAA men and JC/CC collegiate women.

Kills Per Game

This statistic gives an average number of kills scored by a player or team per game. The kills per game statistic does not take hitting errors into consideration. It is important to note that teams which win matches in three or four games (out of five) normally have higher kills per game averages than teams which play a lot of five-game matches. Use the following formula to compute kills per game:

computing kills per game
total kills (K)/number of games played (GP)=kills per game (K/G)

Using the raw data found in Figure 2-6, it is possible to compute the kills per game for Donnell, Lushine and Benning. It is necessary to know the number of games played and the total number of kills. The Official Score Sheet can be consulted if there is a question about the number of games played. Donnell scored eight kills in five games, so eight divided by five equals 1.6 kills per game. Lushine scored six kills and played in only four games. Her kills per game total is 1.5 (6/4 = 1.5). Benning scored 10 kills and played in all five games. Her kills per game is 2.0 (10/5 = 2.0). To compute the team's kills per game, add the kills accumulated by all of the players on the team and divide the kills by the number of games in the match. For example, if the team scored 68 kills in five games, it would have averaged 13.6 kills per game. Season averages are computed by dividing the total number of kills (or

any other skill statistic) by the total number of games played.

Individual Blocking

This statistic gives the number of rally ending blocks participated in by an individual player in each game. Only block solos and block assists, as defined earlier, are used in compiling blocking averages. Although blocking errors are customarily recorded, these errors are not used in calculating either team or individual blocking averages. The following formula is used to calculate an individual player's average:

computing individual blocking averages
(total # BS) + (total # BA) / total # games played = blocks/game (B/G)
BS + BA are commonly referred to as total blocks (TB)

Team Blocking

Different formulas are used for calculating individual and team blocking averages. When computing team blocking averages it is necessary to divide the block assists (BA) by two. Since a block assist is awarded to at least two players for the action of blocking one attack, the data would be skewed without this adjustment. This modification produces a more accurate picture of the number of actual blocks the team earned during a specific game. Use the following formula to calculate the average number of team blocks per game:

computing team blocking averages
(total #BS) + (total # BA)/2 / total # games played = blocks/game (B/G)
Note: only 1/2 of the total block assists are added in calculating team averages.

Figure 2-7 shows an example of blocking statistics which have been accumulated during a single season. The individual player and team averages have been calculated using the above formulas. Figure 2-7 shows that Jeffer accumu-

Figure 2-7: Blocking Chart - Computing Averages

Player	GP	BS	BA	BE
Patterson	74	1	34	7
Pearman	68	5	31	3
Williams	70	2	14	1
McDonnell	56	2	7	5
Jeffer	73	14	71	6
Mason	74	10	81	5
Winston	61	0	13	9
Wong	61	0	3	0
totals	**74**	**34**	**254**	**36**

GP = games played; BS = block solo; BA = block assist; BE = block error; B/G = blocks per game

lated 14 block solos (BS) and 71 block assists (BA) while playing in 73 games. Jeffer's average blocks per game is calculated by adding 14 BS and 71 BA, then dividing that total by 73 games played. Applying the formula to find Jeffer's individual blocking average looks like this:

(14 + 71)/73 = 85/73 = 1.16 blocks per game

Figure 2-7 also shows that the team had a total of 34 block solos (BS) and 254 block assists (BA). To calculate the team average blocks per game, add the total block solos (43) to one-half of the total block assists (127). Next, divide this figure by the number of games played by the team. The complete team calculation looks like this:

34 + (254/2)/74 = (34 + 127)/74

161 / 74 = 2.18 blocks per game

Assists Per Game

This statistic gives an average for the number of assists awarded to a player in each game. Assists are recorded on the AVCA Worksheet or another appropriate form. The assist average may be calculated for any player, but its significance is most directly related to setters. There may be times when the coach is also interested in the assist average for the right side player (alternate setter/opposite) in a 5-1 offense. Compute the assist average with the following formula:

---
computing assist average
total number of assists (A)/total games played (GP) = assists per game (A/G)

For example, at the end of a five-game match, the setter has a total of 63 assists. To calculate the assist average, divide 63 assists by five (games). This setter would have averaged 12.6 assists per game for this match.

Assist Percentage/Efficiency

This statistic provides a percentage

for the number of sets (assist attempts) which result in a kill. Remember, a set can be any attempt (e.g., forearm pass) to put the ball into a position for an attack attempt. Assist percentage is not a commonly used statistic because it is labor intensive to record all attempts. Some volleyball experts also question the validity of the assist percentage. However, it is used by some sport governing bodies as another method for evaluating setters. The assist percentage/efficiency for the setter is comparable to the hitter's kill efficiency. The formula used to determine the assist percentage is as follows:

---
computing assist percentage/efficiency
number of assists (A)/number of assist attempts (ATT) = assist percentage (A%)

If calculating the assist efficiency at the end of a match, take the total assists and divide by the number of attempts. For example, at the end of a match, a setter has 63 assists and attempted 185 assists. This setter would have an assist efficiency of 63/185, or .341. This means that approximately 34 percent of the set attempts resulted in kills.

Digs Per Game

This statistic gives a per game average for successful plays of the opponent's attack attempts. Remember, digs are only awarded for plays of attack attempts (including tips and dumps), not serve reception, free balls or deflections off a block. Digs are simply recorded by tallies on the AVCA Worksheet or another appropriate statistical form and then totaled at the end of a game and/or match. When keeping game statistics on a single worksheet, it would be advisable to use different colored pens for each game. The formula used to compute digs per game is as follows:

---
computing digs
total digs (D)/number of games played (GP) = digs per game (D/G)

At the end of a four-game match, a player has a total of 14 digs. To calculate this player's digs per game, divide the 14 digs by four (games). The average would be 3.5 digs per game.

Reporting Options
Individual Hitting Graph - Appendix, Form 11

This graph is used to plot an individual player's hitting efficiency through the season. The coach can also add a line to plot the kill efficiency. It provides a

visual overview of performance trends. Figure 2-8 shows an example of such a chart for one player, Peterson. The op-

Figure 2-8: Individual Hitting Graph - Hitting Efficiency vs. Kill Percentage

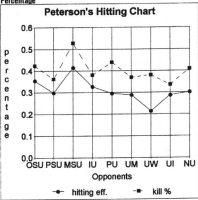

ponents are entered on the horizontal axis. Hitting efficiencies from each match are plotted and connected with lines to show the performance levels. The graph can be completed by the individual player or by a manager. Goals can be set for hitting efficiency and also plotted on the graph before the match. Downward variances in performance should be cause for concern by the coach.

Team Hitting Graph - Appendix, Form 12

The team hitting graph is another visual display of team performance related to hitting efficiency. Opponents are listed on the horizontal axis and team hitting efficiencies are plotted on the graph. The opponent's hitting percentage can also be plotted for comparison. Since hitting efficiency correlates highly with success, the coach should be able to get some idea about minimal efficiency levels necessary to win.

Figure 2-9 (page 20) shows a depiction of one team's hitting efficiencies vs. the opponents over a period of nine matches. Included on the horizontal axis after the team name is a "w" (win) or an "l" (loss). An examination of this chart reveals that it may be necessary for the Minnesota team to hit above a percentage of .250 to win the conference title. (Many other factors can influence wins and losses, but this is one tool that can be very useful to coaches.)

Individual vs. Team Hitting Graph - Appendix, Form 13

This combination graph shows both the team hitting efficiency and an individual player's hitting efficiency for each match. Coaches will find it interesting

Figure 2-9: Team vs. Opponents - Hitting Graph

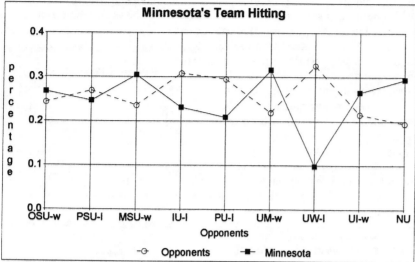

Minnesota's Team Hitting

and enlightening to compare the two performances. Figure 2-10 shows Peterson's hitting performance with the team performance in each match. The coach can check to see if there is any correlation between a specific player's hitting efficiency and the success of the team.

Individual Hitting and Blocking Summary Chart - *Appendix, Form 14*

The Individual Summary Chart provides a chronological display of a single player's hitting and blocking performance. The manager can complete the sections with the date, opponent and site. Before the match the player and/or coach can set performance goals in both areas. After the match the manager completes the match statistics and fills in the averages and totals for the player. Note that the column for W or L (Win/Loss) also has space to write the total number of games played in the match, which is informa-

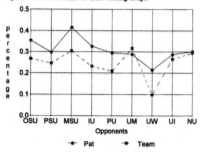

Figure 2-10: Individual vs. Team Hitting Graph

tion needed to calculate averages. This chart is an excellent tool for helping players set realistic goals and focus on achieving them. Keep the form in a notebook provided to the player, or if the coach desires, it can be posted on

the team bulletin board.

Figure 2-11 shows a partially completed hitting and blocking chart for Shaw. In the first match against UM Sept. 2, Shaw's goals are to earn six total blocks

Figure 2-11: Abbreviated Individual Hitting and Blocking Summary

Name: Shaw				BLOCKING					HITTING				
Date	Opponent	W/L	Site	Goal	B/GM	TB	BA	BS	Goal	TA	K	E	Eff.	K%
9/2	UM	W4	home	6	1.25	5	3	2	.300	27	10	3	.259	.370
9/5	OSU	W5	home	6	1.4	7	5	2	.300	31	12	2	.323	.387
9/6	PSU	L4	home	7	1.2	6	4	1	.310	29	9	3	.206	.310
9/12	IU	L4	away	7	1.75	5	5	0	.300	25	8	1	.280	.320

and hit .300 for the match. His actual blocking totals were three block assists and two block solos for a total of five blocks. The five total blocks are divided by four games played to arrive at 1.25 blocks per game. In the hitting area, Shaw had 10 kills, three errors and 27 total attempts. His hitting efficiency calculates to .259, while his kill percentage is .370 (37 percent) for the match. Although Shaw did not meet his blocking or hitting goals in the first match, he surpassed both goals in the second match vs. OSU.

Team Hitting and Blocking Summary Chart - *Appendix, Form 15*

In the Team Summary Chart for hitting and blocking, it is possible to see the entire team's performance at a glance. The team can participate in setting the match goals with the coach giving valuable input and direction during the process. The chart is completed similarly to the individual chart. One important difference is the method used to calculate total blocks for the team—remember, the block assists must be divided in half when calculating team blocks.

Figure 2-12 shows a team summary through four matches. In the first match against UM Sept. 2, the team had six block solos and 13 block assists for a total of 12.5 team blocks (13/2 = 6.5 + 6 = 12.5). The team did not meet its goal of 20 total blocks. However, Minnesota's team hitting goal of .280 was easily accomplished with a stellar .310 hitting efficiency. The team had 158 attempts, 66 kills and 17 hitting errors. The kill percentage is .417, which means that approximately 42 percent of the attack attempts resulted in kills.

Data Interpretation
Hitting Efficiency vs. Kill Percentage

There are many ways to use the data attained from attack statistics. One of the most important tasks the coach has is to determine which hitters are the most efficient scorers. A comparison chart showing both the hitting efficiency and the kill percentage/efficiency for the team's leading hitters can be helpful. Quite a lot of information can be gleaned from this type of chart, as shown in Figure 2-13. Once the coach has digested the statistical information, it would be helpful to share it with the team's setter. Appropriate strategy recommendations should go along with the information. It is important to look at both the hitting efficiency and the kill percentage to give the setter as much information as possible, thereby helping him/her make good set selections.

For example, in Figure 2-13, one sees that Mitchell and Bishop have about the same number of kills and almost identical hitting percentages/efficiency. However, Mitchell has a much higher kill percentage than Bishop, meaning that Mitchell has a better chance of getting a kill. Nevelle is receiving the most sets and has the best efficiency and the best kill percentage. Nevelle should continue to get a large percentage of the sets, especially in critical situations. Becker, on the other hand, is getting far too many sets based on her low efficiency and low kill percentage. This coach should make some strong recommendations to the setter of this team. The observations and

Figure 2-12: Abbreviated Team Summary - Hitting and Blocking Chart

Minnesota				BLOCKING					HITTING					
Date	Opponent	W/L	Site	Goal	B/GM	TB	BA	BS	Goal	TA	K	E	Eff.	K%
9/2	UM	W4	home	20	3.38	12.5	13	6	.280	158	66	17	.310	.417
9/5	OSU	W5	home	20	2.8	14	18	5	.280	184	75	21	.293	.408
9/6	PSU	L4	home	20	2.38	9.5	15	2	.285	143	49	16	.231	.343
9/12	IU	L4	away	20	3.13	12.5	17	4	.285	151	45	8	.245	.298

Figure 2-13: Hitting Efficiency vs. Kill Percentage

Player	TA	K	E	Eff.	K%
Nevelle	1067	461	119	0.321	0.432
Mitchell	623	235	97	0.222	0.377
Becker	955	230	113	0.123	0.241
Bishop	957	231	19	0.221	0.242
Fiamengo	342	152	51	0.295	0.444

recommendations based on the information in Figure 2-13 might look something like this:

Observation	Recommendations
•Nevelle - highest combined efficiency and kill percentage	•Continue setting her a lot; she is our "go to player."
•Fiamengo - high efficiency and high kill percentage	•She needs many more sets--second as "go to player."
•Bishop - Medium to low efficiency and low kill percentage	•Gets far too many sets but she probably will not make many errors under pressure.
•Mitchell - Medium to low efficiency and medium kill percentage	•Give her fewer sets while trying to put her in more one-on-one situations (improve her efficiency).
•Becker - Very low efficiency and low K%	•Use her as a decoy -- do not set her unless absolutely necessary.

AVCA Worksheet

If the coach is using this form to record match statistics on the bench, it is possible to get an overview of how efficiently each hitter is performing. It does not give much detailed information, but just knowing the game-by-game hitting results can be helpful. Figure 2-14 shows data used earlier in this chapter. According to Figure 2-14, Lushine had a slow start in the match, not scoring any kills in the first two games. During game No. 3 she became a "hot hitter," accumulating

four kills in five attempts with no errors. This calculates to a hitting efficiency of .800! Perhaps Lushine should have re-ceived more sets in game No. 3 and throughout the remainder of the match. In game No. 4, Lushine had only three attempts (two kills and one error) and she had no attempts in game No. 5. Benning had a "so-so" match, not really making much of an impact with her .138 hitting efficiency. Lushine's hitting efficiency of .385 was significantly higher than Donnell's .250 efficiency. Unfortunately for the team, Donnell received almost twice as many sets (attempts) as Lushine received. Assuming that no unusual cir-

cumstances surrounded the distribution of these sets, both the coach and the setter should have been aware of these facts during the match. The setter needed to get the ball to the hot hitter and refrain from setting to the lower efficiency hitter.

Attack Chart

The most helpful tool for coaches looking specifically for information about a hitter's performance is the attack chart (sometimes referred to as a shot chart). It is especially helpful because with a quick glance in the heat of the action or during a time-out, the coach can make observations about what is working and what is not. Most importantly, the coach can then give that information to the hitters and the setter. And better yet, the coach can talk about what is working (not what is not working!) while showing the chart to the players. Most players respond much better to visual information than verbal information.

Figure 2-15 (page 22) shows an attack chart for one game during a match. This visual material can be used in the break between games or in a time-out to give the players a considerable amount of good information. Following is a very general example of some "coaching" that could be given to each hitter and the setter while showing them the attack chart:

•Player No. 12 - You are scoring on line shots; keep attacking the line; deep corner shots are also good from the back row.

•Player No. 9 - Shots to your right (cross-court) are scoring; be aware of your position on the court—if you are too close to the right line, do not take a full swing or turn your shoulders into the court; tips are good if you need to use them.

•Player No. 3-setter - You are scoring on dumps but use them sparingly; get all of your sets out to the line (front and back) so the hitters can attack the line; No. 7 (middle hitter) has three kills in four attempts; back-row attacks have scored

Figure 2-14: Abbreviated AVCA Worksheet

Player	No	Game 1	Game 2	Game 3	Game 4	Game 5	K	E	TA	EFF.
Donnell	11	kkkoe	ook	kooo	oeokook	koooo	8	2	24	0.25
Lushine	8	ooo	oo	okkkk	ekk		6	1	13	0.385
Benning	15	okkoe	ooookek	kooee	okokkke	ookooe	10	6	29	0.138

Game Totals	Kills	Errors	Attempts	EFF.	Attack Key:
1	5	2	13	0.231	0 = attack (stays in play)
2	3	1	11	0.182	k = kill
3	6	2	14	0.286	e = error
4	8	3	17	0.294	TA = o + e + k
5	2	1	11	0.091	PCT. = k - e / Attempts

Figure 2-15: Sample Attack Chart

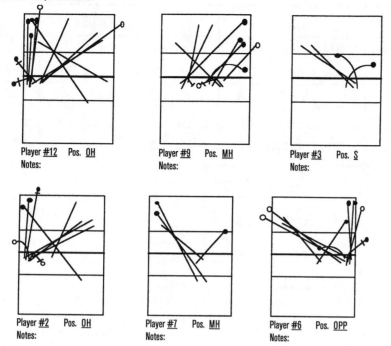

Player #12   Pos. OH
Notes:

Player #9   Pos. MH
Notes:

Player #3   Pos. S
Notes:

Player #2   Pos. OH
Notes:

Player #7   Pos. MH
Notes:

Player #6   Pos. OPP
Notes:

every time.

•Player No. 2 - Keep hitting line shots, they are scoring better than cross-court shots; you will probably get some more back-row sets—go to the corners.

•Player No. 7 - Good back-row attacks—keep going to the deep corners; when you get more quick-sets, keep hitting power (cross-court).

•Player No. 6 - Your sets are going to be out to the line—get your shoulders square and keep hitting line where you are scoring; hit any combination play-sets back cross-court.

Coaches also need to keep some form of an attack chart on the opponents during the match. By showing the team the opponent's chart, a coach can assist the players in making adjustments on the court to reduce the effectiveness of the opponent's offense. For example, if the chart in Figure 2-15 represented the opponent's attack chart, the coach may have the following comments about blocking and defense:

•Block line -

The opponents are scoring most of their kills down both sidelines—outside blocker turn your hands into the court to prevent wipe-offs.

•Adjust the defense - Move a digger to the deep corners on the line to dig (especially if the line blockers are weak or small).

•Drop the defense to the deep corners on back-row attacks - Back-row hitters are hitting the deep, cross-court corners.

•Left front hitter help block quick middle attacks - Their middle hitters are having success hitting power—take the angle away.

•Read the hitters and setter for tips - Left back and right back charge to dig tips.

Blocking

At higher levels of play, the ability of a team to stop the opponent's attack at the net is critical to its success. As hitters become stronger and better, it is a formidable task to execute a controlled dig from a great attack. Most coaches agree that blocking is one of the most difficult skills to teach—or at least teaching players to be successful blockers is difficult! There are as many blocking strategies in volleyball as there are defensive systems. Some coaches are content to have blockers slow the ball down (control or soft block) as it passes over the net off an attack. Others want the blockers to give the hitter a funnel or alley into which they can attack, where back-court defensive players are positioned, ready to dig the ball. Still others want the blockers to go for the ball and stop it before it crosses the net. The type of system a coach uses is not as important as having a definite blocking strategy or tactics which the team understands and with which they can be successful.

Although blocking errors are customarily recorded, these errors are not used in calculating either team or individual blocking averages. Most coaches keep track of their own team's blocking errors because these errors result in either the loss of a point for their team or a side-out. As a coach, it is important to know how many rally ending errors per game your team is committing. A large num-

Figure 2-16: Attack and Block Chart

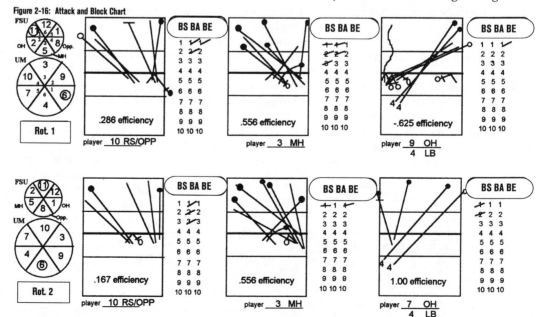

ber of individual or team errors related to any one skill are a cause for concern and should lead to extra practice time in that area.

A real plus for a coach is to have blockers who are reasonably good at "reading the hitter" so the block is positioned in the appropriate area. Hitters, on the other hand, have to know the blocking strengths of the team they are facing—who is strong or weak and who is quick or slow? Knowing the blocking schemes and defensive systems used by the opponents will also help the hitters to be successful. The setter must then be able to deliver a set which gives the hitter a better chance of being successful. During a match, a tool like the Attack and Block Chart can give the coach some valuable information. It will show how well the team is performing in attacking and blocking and give some insight into making the right decisions about the team's rotational order for upcoming games. Figure 2-16 shows two rotations with attack charts and blocking totals for Minnesota (UM). In a regular match there would, of course, be six rotations. For purposes of this example, only two rotations are being examined—with more information, the conclusions might be different. There are many ways to analyze the data, but one way would be to look at the match-ups with hitters vs. blockers. Assume the Minnesota outside hitters (OH) face the FSU opposite hitters (OPP or RS); the Minnesota middle hitters (MH) face the FSU middle hitters; and the Minnesota opposites face the FSU outside hitters in each rotation. The middle hitters hopefully can help block on both the right and left sides. Back-row attacks will not be considered in this example. Following is a hitting and blocking summary with the match-ups as they appear in Figure 2-16:

you are only looking at these two rotations, the information is somewhat limited, but some definite observations can be noted. UM's coach might decide that the outside hitter No. 9 is having a difficult time being successful (both hitting and blocking) against FSU's No. 8 (OPP), but everyone else is doing well. This is probably a good match-up since UM's outside hitter No. 9 will only face FSU's No. 8 in one out of the three rotations she is in the front row. If other players were unsuccessful, the UM coach might want to rotate one or two rotations before starting the next game (i.e., have No. 3 or No. 7 serve first). For an even more detailed analysis of the UM hitters, the coach could calculate the hitter's attack efficiency in each rotation. Some computer software will do this as part of the program.

Set Selection

Although assists are kept primarily as a media statistic, many governing bodies require the reporting of assists for post-season honors. Assists should be tallied for all players, but it is primarily the setter and/or right side players who will earn a majority of the assists. In essence, the assist statistic has become primarily a "setter's statistic." Clearly, the ability of the setter to deliver a good set which results in a kill is influenced by many factors:

•accuracy of the team's pass from serve reception, free ball or a transition dig;

•availability of hitters—are they ready and in position to approach and hit;

•current rotation—hitters and options available to the setter;

•opponent's defense—strength and position of the opposing blockers and back-court players;

•ability of the hitter to be successful. Volleyball enthusiasts should be cau-

method. Consequently, assists have evolved into more of a statistic used by the media to describe setters rather than a coaching statistic used to evaluate the ability of a setter. One of the tools used by coaches in evaluating the performance of setters is a form similar to the one shown in Figure 2-17, page 24 (the Set Selection Chart, described earlier in this chapter). The data recorded on the chart represents the data found on the Attack and Block Chart shown in Figure 2-16.

The notations in Figure 2-17 (page 24) show the chronological distribution of the sets in rotation Nos. 1 and 2. The "notes" section gives a summary of each hitter's performance, the setter's performance and the passing performance of the team. The "summary" gives the hitting efficiency in each rotation, a brief description of the most and least successful plays, and some comments about what the statistician noticed. Even though this example includes only two rotations, the coach can communicate some definite positive and negative tendencies for the setter:

•middle hitter No. 3 was very effective on almost all sets—especially with the slide (this could be due to a weak blocker(s) or the skill of the hitter);

•outside hitter No. 9 struggled against the block—perhaps the setter could set her when passes were perfect, rather than only on "1" or "2" passes (if No. 9 is normally a better hitter, this is a cause for further study);

•outside hitter No. 7 was scoring but only got two sets—give her more (setters sometimes get discouraged from setting one position if the last hitter was unsuccessful in that position);

•the setter rarely sets the middle on "2" passes—when this happens, the opponent's middle blocker tends to release to the outside, setting up a double block for the outside hitter (this could be part of No. 9's problem);

•the back-row attacks (A's) to No. 4 were generally very effective—perhaps this is an option which should be used more often, especially if No. 9 is struggling.

Can you identify other tendencies and make coaching comments to this setter?

Rotation	Minnesota		FSU	UM Hitting	UM Blocking
1	OH No. 9	vs.	Opp. No. 8	poor - 0K, 5E	poor - 1 BE
	MH No. 3	vs.	MH No. 5	good - 6K, 1E	good - 5 TB
	OPP No. 10	vs.	OH No. 2	average - 3K, 1E	average - 2BA
2	OH No. 7	vs.	OPP No. 8	good - 2K, 2TA	good - 2BS
	MH No. 3	vs.	MH No. 5	good - 6K, 1E	average - 2TB
	OPP No. 10	vs.	OH No. 1	average, 2K, 1E	good - 3BA

So, what does this mean? This information would be particularly helpful if Minnesota and FSU are scheduled to play each other in the near future. Since

tioned against judging setters based exclusively on assist statistics. If one considers the factors listed above, it is easy to understand why this is not a very reliable

Summary
Digs

The emphasis on hitting and blocking has sometimes overshadowed the importance of back-court defense, specifi-

Figure 2-17: Abbreviated Set Selection Chart

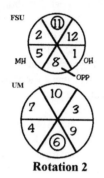

Rotation 1

Pass	Set	Result		Pass	Set	Result		Pass	Set	Result	
1. 3	52/10/+	K	11. 2	14/9/+	B	21. 3	52/10/o	E
2. 2	93/10/o	O	12. 3	94/3/+	K	22. 3	92/3/+	K
3. 3	51/3/+	K	13. 2	14/9/o	O	23. 1	14/9/o	O
4. 1	95/10/+	K/B	14. 2	A/4/+	K	24. 1	14/9/o	E
5. 2	31/3/-	B/NE	15. 3	92/3/+	K	25. 3	51/3/+	K
6. 3	51/3/+	O	16. 1	15/9/o	B	26. 2	92/3/o	K
7. 2	92/10/o	O	17. 3	92/3/+	K	27. 2	93/9/o	B
8. 2	BHE	---	18. 1	A/4/o	K	28. 2	92/3/+	K
9. 3	52/10/+	E	19. 2	52/10/o	O	29. 3	51/3/o	O
10. 2	14/9/+	B	20. 2	14/9/o	O	30.		

Notes

#	K	E		TA	%
10	3	1		7	.286
3	6	1		9	.556
9	0	5		8	-.625
4	2	0		2	1.00

setter:

+	o	-	E
14	13	1	1

passing:

3	2	1	0
11	13	5	0

Rotation 2

Pass	Set	Result		Pass	Set	Result		Pass	Set	Result	
1. 3	52/10/+	K	11. 2	14/7/o	K	21.		
2. 2	92/10/o	O	12. 2	92/3/o	O	22.		
3. 3	51/3/+	K	13. 2	A/4/o	K	23.		
4. 1	95/10/+	O	14. 1	92/3/+	K	24.		
5. 2	51/3/o	K	15. 3	92/3/+	K	25.		
6. 3	51/3/-	K	16. 3	92/3/-	O	26.		
7. 2	92/10/o	O	17. 2	94/10/+	K	27.		
8. 2	14/7/+	K	18. 2	92/3/-	B	28.		
9. 3	52/10/o	B	19. 2	92/3/o	K	29.		
10. 2	A/4/x9o	E	20. 0	---	---	30.		

Notes

#	K	E		TA	%
10	2	1		6	.167
3	6	1		9	.556
7	2	0		2	1.00
4	1	1		2	.0

setter:

+	o	-	E
7	9	3	0

passing:

3	2	1	0
6	11	2	1

Key

Pass Ratings:
3 = all options
   (perfect pass)
2 = two options-
   no middle attack
1 = one option
0 = error/RE

Example: 72/3/+

Set Selection:
type/player # /rating

type = area & tempo
   (i.e., 31, 52)

rating : + = good
   0 = average
   - = poor

X(#) = non-setter
   (player number)

Result:
K = kill
E = error
0 = dug
B = blocked/error
BHE = ball handling
   error
NE = net error
CE = centerline
   error

Summary

Rot.	K	E	TA	PCT.	Best Hitter	Least Successful	Best Play	Comments
1	12	8	28	0.14	3 & 4 (A)	#9 - OH -4 set	92 - #3	+ slide, set OH on 3 pass
2	11	3	19	0.42	3 and 7 (14)	#10- OPP	92/51- #3	+ slide, more sets to #7
3								

cally digging. Coaches will agree that while the net game has become increasingly important, it would be foolhardy to ignore how critical defense is to the success of a team. Many coaches feel that team intensity is directly related to the willingness of individual players to exert an all-out effort to dig every ball. A great dig off of a hard-hit attack can spark a team and change the momentum in a match. Coaches often insert a fireball defensive player into a game with the specific intent of changing the chemistry or intensity on the court. A great back-court specialist is like an ace in the hole for coaches—do not overlook the importance of one. (Eric Sato served as a defensive specialist on the U.S. men's national team for many years and he was able to play a major role in many matches.)

Some coaches track (tally) the digs of players in scrimmages. This decision can prove to be valuable in several ways. It can be a motivating factor for players who seem only concerned with their hitting and blocking performance. When players know that the coach is taking notice of defensive play, performance in that area seems to improve. Additionally, keeping records about defensive play can reinforce decisions the coach makes about which players are the best back-row defenders.

What Are Good Averages?
Hitting Efficiencies

As was mentioned earlier, team hitting efficiency is one of the best indicators of success. When the level of play becomes better, the hitting efficiencies normally improve. Better passing at higher levels of play is another factor leading to higher hitting efficiencies. At similar levels of play, males usually have higher hitting percentages than females, due to enhanced jumping ability and upper body strength. Hitting efficiencies for outstanding individual female and male players can range from above .400 to as high as .550, respectively. The following ranges reflect normal hitting efficiencies for good, competitive teams at different levels:

Team	Females	Males
High School/"B" Open	.200-.250	.230-.280
College/"AA" Open	.260-.310	.320-.370
"AAA" Open	.280-.330	.340-.390
International	.290-.350	.350-.400

Kills Per Game

The number of kills per game is usually influenced by the length of the game. Longer games (more rallies and side-outs) normally result in an increased number of kills, thereby increasing the kills per game averages. Top collegiate male and female players normally average six to seven kills per game and these teams normally average 17 to 20 kills per game. The averages for men are frequently slightly higher than those for women because men's games are traditionally longer.

Blocking

Since blocking is one of the most difficult skills to master, it stands to reason that blocking averages for individuals and teams will increase as does the level of play. Again, because of enhanced upper body strength and jumping ability across the board, men may have higher blocking averages than women. At the collegiate level, outstanding male and female players normally average between 1.4 to 1.9 blocks per game. Below are the average number of blocks (per game) for good, competitive teams at varying levels of play.

Team	Females	Males
High School/"B" Open	2.0-3.0	.2.5-3.5
College/"AA" Open	2.9-3.9	.3.6-4.6
"AAA" Open	3.6-4.6	.4.6-5.6
International	4.2-5.2	5.3-6.3

Assists

Individual player and team assist averages increase as the level of competition increases because games are longer with more rallies and kills. The following ranges for assist per game averages are for individual setters in a 5-1 offense. Teams that employ an offense with two or more setters will have averages which are significantly lower.

Team	Females	Males
High School/"B" Open	12.5-14.0	15.5-17.0
College/"AA" Open	13.5-15.0	16.5-18.0
"AAA" Open	14.5-16.0	17.5-19.0
International	16.5-18.0	19.5-21.0

Digs

An outstanding collegiate player will average between four to five digs per game, while an outstanding team may average between 17 to 20 digs per game. The defensive system used by the team will greatly influence the number of digs accumulated by individual players and by the team in general.

Summary

•**Hitting Efficiency** gives a percentage rating of the overall effectiveness (success rate) of the attacks against the opponents. Most experts feel that hitting efficiency is the statistic which correlates most highly with team success. To arrive at the hitting efficiency, subtract the errors from the kills and divide the difference by the total number of attempts. Hitting efficiency is also commonly referred to as the hitting percent or attack percentage.

•**Kill Percentage** gives a percentage rating for the total number of attacks which result directly in a point or side-out. In essence, this rating will tell which hitters are the most "deadly." Errors are not calculated into this formula. If players have approximately the same hitting efficiency, the player with a higher kill percentage is more likely to score a kill.

•**Block Solo** is the term which refers to a single player's action of blocking the ball back into the opponent's court, leading directly to a point or side-out.

•**Block Assist** is used to describe the action of two or more players who block the ball back into the opponent's court for a point or side-out. Each player involved in the attempt to block is awarded a block assist, even if he/she did not actually touch the ball.

•**Blocking Average** for individuals is calculated by adding the total block solos and the total block assists, then dividing the sum by the number of games played.

•**Total Team Blocks** is a statistic which is usually recorded for each team on the Official Box Score at the end of a match. To arrive at this figure, add the total block solos and one-half of the total block assists. The total block assists are divided in half to give a more realistic picture of how many actual blocks took place in the match.

•**Team Blocking Average** is calculated by adding the total block solos and one-half of the total block assists, then dividing the sum by the total number of games. The team blocking average also correlates highly with overall team success, but usually not as highly as hitting efficiency.

•An **assist** is awarded to a player for a set (underhand pass or overhand pass) to a teammate which results in a kill. Although all assists are recorded for the Official Box Score, it is usually only the setter's assists which are significant. Evaluating setter ability should not be based exclusively on assist averages because setting is so dependent upon team passing. Setters are also dependent upon the hitter's ability.

•A **dig** is awarded to a player for the pass of an opponent's attacked ball. The pass of a dump or tip is also considered a dig. In order for the dig to count, the ball must remain in play after the dig. Free balls or balls passed from a deflection off a block are not scored as digs.

Chapter 3

"Creative minds have always been known to survive any kind of bad training." Anna Freud, Sigmund Freud's daughter

The Official Box Score

Volleyball is second only to soccer in worldwide popularity. It has a huge worldwide following of fans and participants at every imaginable level of play, both male and female. In the United States volleyball is the second most popular team sport for collegiate women and high school girls and the number of junior programs for young girls in this country has literally exploded in recent years. Many states have also established boys' high school championships. Although volleyball is not as extensive for collegiate men, there are large numbers of collegiate club teams which augment the intercollegiate level of competition. Despite all of these facts, knowledge about game statistics for volleyball has seemingly remained a mystery to the typical American media personality. Because of the lack of knowledge, enthusiasts have been left to read stories of matches which do an inadequate job of describing the action taking place on the court. Therefore, the challenge appears to be for volleyball coaches and enthusiasts to set forth on a mission to help enlighten the media about statistics used in volleyball.

Whether coaches like to admit it or not, promotion is an important part of the job. Some coaches may be lucky enough to have an individual assigned to provide leadership in the area of promotions. Other coaches may have to take on this responsibility themselves. One of the best ways to promote interest in your team and increase the knowledge of the media and fans who are watching the game is to provide statistics after the match. An understanding of the Official Box Score is a starting point to increase this knowledge base. The box score gives a summary of the action taking place in a typical match and is intended to be a media tool. This chapter describes the Official Volleyball Box Score as it is outlined in the *National Volleyball Statistics Manual*.

The Rating System

The rating system used to complete the AVCA Worksheet and, in turn, the Official Box Score, are described throughout Chapter 2. Refer back for a refresher if necessary. Following are rating systems for the serve, serve reception and ball handling errors, not previously discussed.

The Serve

There are three possible outcomes for every served ball:

•**A service ace (SA)** is a serve which results directly in a point. It is awarded to a player if:
  a. the serve strikes the opponent's court untouched;
  b. the serve is passed by the opponent but cannot be kept in play;
  c. the official calls a violation on the receiver (e.g., lift); or
  d. the receiving team is out of rotation (e.g., overlap).

•**A service error (SE)** is charged to a player if:
  a. the serve hits the net or fails to clear the net;
  b. the serve is out-of-bounds or hits the antenna;
  c. the server foot-faults on the serve or takes too much time; or
  d. the player serves out of rotation–the SE is charged to the player who should have been serving.

•**A zero serve (0)** is a serve which does not result in a service ace or a service error. Documentation of this is only necessary if the statistician is calculating serve percentage.

The Serve Reception

There are three possible outcomes when a player(s) attempts to pass a successful serve:

•**A reception error (RE)** is charged to a player if:
  a. the serve strikes the floor in the area of the player;
  b. the player passes the serve but it cannot be kept in play by his/her team; or

  c. the player is called for a reception violation by the official (e.g., lift).

•**A zero service reception (0)** occurs when a player continues play by successfully passing a served ball and the pass does not result in a kill or lead directly to a kill by a teammate. Documentation of this is only necessary if the statistician is calculating serve reception percentage.

•**A team reception error (TRE)** is awarded when:
  a. a serve falls between two players and the statistician cannot determine which player was responsible; or
  b. when the receiving team was out of rotation.

Ball Handling

•**A ball handing error (BHE)** is recorded any time the official blows the whistle, ending play, and calls:
  •a double hit;
  •a thrown ball; or
  •a lifted ball.

Exceptions to the ball handling error include:
  •a double hit called on serve reception is a reception error (RE), not a BHE;
  •a thrown ball during an attack is an attack error (E); or
  •a thrown ball during a block is a blocking error (BE).

Recording Options
AVCA Worksheet - Appendix, Form 7

The first step to completing the Official Box Score is to record the events of the match on the AVCA Worksheet. (A detailed explanation of how to complete the AVCA Worksheet was previously discussed.) Refer to the section "recording options" in Chapter 2, Figure 2-1, to find the discussion and examples of how to complete this form manually. Many computerized statistical programs are also available for taking statistics during matches. These programs allow the statistician to input data while the match is in progress and automatically compile a summary at the end of each game and another at the end of the match. Some of these computer programs will produce a completed box score at the conclusion of the match.

The Statistics Crew

The coach needs to find several people who have an interest in the game and teach them the basic terminology and definitions provided in this chapter. (An excellent resource for statistics crew members is the *AVCA National Statistic Manual* and the AVCA "Statistics Videotape." Both provide even more examples of how to classify specific situations which occur during competition.)

The statistics crew is usually comprised of at least three people: Two people who record data for each team and the third person, who acts as the "caller." The caller verbally describes the match while the "recorders" transcribe the data onto the worksheet. If the statistics crew is inexperienced, it might help to have one caller for each team. To aid the statistics crew in becoming accustomed to the system, invite them into daily practices. While the team is scrimmaging, the crew can work on perfecting its statistics taking skills. Most statistics crews will develop their own style of calling and recording.

Actions which result in a dead ball (kills, blocks, service errors, reception errors, hitting errors, blocking errors and ball handling errors) are usually easy to record because of the break in the action. Accurately recording attacks which remain in play, assists and digs will take more practice.

Computing Options
Hitting Efficiency

Computing the hitting efficiency for the box score uses the same formula as found in Chapter 2. As a reminder, the hitting efficiency tells what percentage of the attacks led directly to a point or a side-out and considers attacking errors as part of the equation. To calculate the hitting efficiency, subtract the errors from the kills and divide by the total attempts (refer to page 17 for the complete formula). Additionally, different formulas are used to calculate individual and team blocking, which will also be discussed in this chapter. (Please refer to page 18 for refresher

information regarding computing team blocking averages.)

Team Attacks Per Game

This area under each team roster on the Official Box Score is provided to give the team's attacking totals in kills, errors, total attacks and hitting percentage for each game. From the worksheet the statistician totals the number of kills, errors and total attempts for all players on the team during the specific game. With these totals it is possible to calculate the team hitting percentage for each game. If separate worksheets are used for each game, the process is easier. When only one worksheet is used for the entire match, the statistician should use different colored pens to distinguish the games. There is usually enough time between games for the statistician to compile the statistics in this section.

Totaling the Other Areas

All of the other categories in the box score are simply a sum of the statistics in each area. For example, add each player's tallies under the dig area of the worksheet and record that total in the line for each player under the dig column. To get the team totals, add each player's number of digs and put the total on the bottom line for "team totals" under the dig column. The same method is used for every category.

Reporting Options
Official AVCA Box Score - Appendix, Form 16

This form gives a statistical summary of the action during a volleyball match. As was mentioned earlier, the box score is primarily intended to be a tool used by the media for reporting the highlights of a match. In essence, the box score reports all rally ending plays (e.g., kills, blocks, aces, etc.) in a match and additionally gives statistics about digs and assists. As was mentioned earlier, it is essential that we provide the media with this statistical information about the match. We want to educate and encourage them to write stories with substantive statistical information about the match, not just fluff! Coaches need to find a way to gather and disseminate match statistics in an effort to ensure accurate and noteworthy reporting.

Figure 3-1 shows an example of a completed AVCA Box Score. The box score can easily be completed after the

match by transferring the raw data from the AVCA Worksheet. The Box Score includes statistics from all skill areas and gives a very good overview of the entire match. Some of the highlights of this box score include:

• The starters for each team are signified by the "s" following their name on the roster.

• The starters for North Central were Mason, Smith, Johanson, Pederson, Wells and Wilson.

• Kennedy won the match in four games—15-13, 12-15, 15-8, 15-7.

• The leading hitter for North Central was Johanson, with 11 kills and a .500 hitting efficiency. Wells had more kills (13), but had only a .128 hitting efficiency.

• Kennedy had a more balanced attack, with three players scoring kills in double figures and recording hitting efficiencies above .250.

• Kennedy won the hitting battle with a .261 team attack percentage vs. North Central's .219 efficiency. Note that a comparison between the number of kills and attempts for each team was very close, but North Central had more hitting errors.

• In the blocking areas, North Central had 12 team blocks, while Kennedy had eight team blocks. Individually, Wilson for North Central led all blockers in the match with seven total blocks.

• In the digs category, Keefe for Kennedy led all players with 21 digs and the Kennedy team "out-dug" North Central, 71 to 59 digs.

• Langley for Kennedy had four service aces, leading all players. The Kennedy team had 10 aces, while North Central had only five aces.

This is an example of how helpful the box score can be in providing facts for the media about the match. A person would not even have to see the match to write a story!

Abbreviated or Short Box Score

Most members of the print media will not want to reproduce an entire box score in stories about a match. Several sports have developed an abbreviated box score format as a substitute for the complete box. The AVCA has developed an abbreviated box or short box score to be used for volleyball. Introduce this concept to the media in your area and encourage them to use it. Only game scores and point scoring events or statistics are used in the short box score.

OFFICIAL AVCA BOX SCORE

Site: Center City　　　　Date: Oct. 12, 1998　　　　Attendance: 4637

TEAM North Central			ATTACK				SET	SERVE			DEF	BLOCK			GEN
No.	Player	GP	K	E	TA	PCT.	A	SA	SE	RE	DIG	BS	BA	BE	BHE
1	Johnson, K	4	2	3	11	-9			1		6				
2	Mason, L s	4	2	3	8	-125	44	1	2		9		2	1	3
3	Smith, B s	4	11	5	29	207	2	1	1	1	7	1	2		2
4	Mattson, F	4	0	0	1	0				3	2				
5	Miller, S	1					1								
6	Olson, T	2	2	2	9	0	1	1		1	2				
7	Clup, A														
8	Johanson, R s	4	11	1	20	500			1	2	5	1	1		
9	McDonald, S	3	0	0	0	0									
10	Pederson, M s	4	11	2	22	409	2	1	3		5		4		1
11	Wells, L s	4	13	8	39	128		1		2	20		4		1
12	Wilson, E s	4	10	3	21	333	2		1	1	3		7		
TEAM TOTALS:			62	27	160	219	52	5	9	10	59	2	20	1	7

Team Attack Per Game:　　　　Team RE: 0　　Total Team Blocks: 12

Gm	K	E	TA	Pct.	Pts	Game Scores	1	2	3	4	5	Team Records
1	17	16	42	262	13	North Central	13	15	8	7		18-10 (conf. 9-7)
2	15	33	38	316	15							
3	13	4	3	273	8							
4	17	14	47	64	7	Kennedy	15	12	15	15		20-7 (conf. 12-3)
5												

TEAM Kennedy			ATTACK				SET	SERVE			DEF	BLOCK			GEN
No.	Player	GP	K	E	TA	PCT.	A	SA	SE	RE	DIG	BS	BA	BE	BHE
3	Franco, D s	4	14	5	35	257	4	2	1	2	9		1	1	
4	Langley, V s	4	8	4	20	200		4			8		1		
5	Keefe, L s	4	13	3	31	323	2		1	1	17	1			2
6	Manderfeld, M s	4	18	7	41	268		1	1		10	1	1		1
8	Brendan, P														
9	Macias, P	4										1	1		
10	Wilson, D														
11	Robertson, D s	4	3	2	12	83	49	3			15	2			5
12	Schneider, T s	4	8	2	18	333	1				12		2		
13	Reed, T														
14	Nelson, K														
TEAM TOTALS:			64	23	157	261	56	10	3	3	71	5	6	1	8

Team Attack Per Game:　　　　Team RE: 2　　Total Team Blocks: 8

Gm	K	E	TA	Pct.	Pts	
1	13	7	39	154	15	Length of Match: 1:53
2	16	6	45	222	12	First Referee: Kathy Williamson
3	17	5	45	387	15	Second Referee: Tom Michelson
4	18	5	42	310	15	Notes:　　yellow card Kennedy coach - gm 2
5						

Key:
A = Assists　　GP = Games Played
K = Kills　　TA = Total Attempts
E = Errors　　Pct = %

BHE = Ball Handling Errors
RE = Receiving Errors
SA = Block Solos
BA = Block Assists

SA = Service Ace
SE = Service Error
Team Blocks = BS + 1/2 BA
Team RE = RE not assigned to any one player

Kill Pct = (K - E) / TA
D = Digs
BE = Block Errors

Figure 3-2: Abbreviated or Short Box Score - North Central vs. Kennedy

Kennedy def. North Central 15-13, 12-15, 15-8, 15-7
North Central (18-10) (Kills-Aces-Blocks) Johnson 2-0-0; Mason 2-1-2; Smith 11-1-3; Mattson 0-0-0; Miller 0-0-0; Olson 2-1-0; Johanson 11-0-2; McDonald 0-0-0; Pederson 11-1-4; Wells 13-1-4; Wilson 10-0-7; Totals 62-5-12.
Kennedy (20-7) Franco 14-2-1; Langley 8-4-1; Keefe 13-0-1; Manderfeld 18-1-2; Macias 0-0-2; Robertson 3-3-2; Schneider 8-0-2; **Totals** 64-10-8. Length of Match: 1:53; Attendance 4,637.

Figures 3-2 and 3-3 show abbreviated box score formats for the match just described, North Central vs. Kennedy. In the short box score, the team scores are listed with the team records. Then kills, aces and blocks are listed for each player who participates in any part of the match. Finally, the team totals for kills, aces and blocks are listed. As a point of interest,

Figure 3-3: Alternate Format Short Box Score
15-13, 12-15, 15-8, 15-7

North Central	Kills	Aces	Blocks
Johnson	2	0	0
Mason	2	1	2
Smith	11	1	3
Mattson	0	0	0
Miller	0	0	0
Olson	2	1	0
Johanson	11	0	2
McDonald	0	0	0
Pederson	11	1	4
Wells	13	1	4
Wilson	10	0	7
Totals	62	5	12
Kennedy			
Franco	14	2	1
Langley	8	4	1
Keefe	13	0	1
Manderfeld	18	1	2
Macias	0	0	2
Robertson	3	3	2
Schneider	8	0	2
Totals	64	10	8
Attendance–4,637		Length of Match 1:53	

the length of the match and the attendance have been added.

Data Interpretation

Since the box score is primarily intended for use by the media, it has limited value to coaches other than providing a summary of the match statistics. Other charts and forms described in this manual provide the coach with better definitive information about the performance of the team vs. the opponents. However, in a pinch, the box score can serve as a source for a rough scouting report on a team you may be preparing to play. If you have access to the opponent's cumulative season statistics, your observations become even more valuable. With careful examination of the box score (and the season totals, if available), one can usually determine:

•the number of setters reveals the

type of offense (shows the number of setters receiving a significant number of assists);

•who the primary setter is (most assists);

•the best hitters (number of attack attempts and hitting efficiency);

•the weak hitters (low number of attack attempts and/or low hitting percentage);

•the best blockers (blocking totals);

•the most dangerous servers and less consistent servers (service aces and errors);

•the weak passers (reception errors) — this may also indicate players who receive the most passing attempts and therefore naturally have more errors;

•the outside hitters (usually most attack attempts);

•the middle hitters (usually the most blocks);

•the right side/opposite players (usually the most block assists and second in assists);

•a good guess at the rotation order. Traditionally, in a 5-1 offense, the setter is surrounded by the best outside hitter (OH1) and the best middle hitter (MH1). This is done because the coach normally wants the best two hitters in the front row for the maximum number of rotations when the setter, a non-hitting player, is in the front row. For this reason, the hitters surrounding the setter normally receive more attack attempts. The opposite (right-side hitter) is therefore positioned opposite the setter in the rotation order. Then the coach can fill in the second outside hitter (OH2) opposite of OH1 and the second middle hitter (MH2) opposite MH1.

If we take the box score from the North Central vs. Kennedy match, it is possible to put these theories to the test. Having season cumulative statistical totals for the team can make the task more simple, but it is possible to arrive at a good "guestimate" without them. Figure 3-4 shows the cumulative season statistical totals for the Kennedy team. They will be used to reinforce the process of determining the probable rotation order for Kennedy.

From the cumulative statistics in Figure 3-4 and the box score in Figure 3-1, the following observations can be made about the likely rotation order Kennedy will use. Keep in mind that it is always the coach's prerogative to change the rotation order, but it is uncommon for a coach to change the actual rotational order in the middle of a season. The coach may start the game with a different player serving (this is called spinning the wheel), but the basic placement of the players within the rotation should not and usually does not change from match to match. Once players get used to a rotation order and the adjacent players, it is difficult for them to have this relationship rearranged. Following are the observations about Kennedy's line-up derived from studying the statistics:

•Keefe (No. 5) and Manderfeld (No. 6) have the most attack attempts—they are probably the hitters surrounding the setter.

•Robertson (No. 11) is the setter in a 5-1 offense (most assists).

•Manderfeld is one of the leading blockers and is therefore probably a middle blocker—possibly MH1.

•Schneider (No. 12) is the leading blocker and probably the other middle blocker—MH2.

•Keefe must be an outside hitter (OH1) if Manderfeld is a middle hitter.

•Franco (No. 3) is probably the opposite (OPP), since she has a large number of assists and also a high number of attack attempts.

•Langley (No. 4) should be the other outside hitter (OH2) because she also has a high number of attack attempts.

Figure 3-5 shows a diagram of probable rotation order for Kennedy based upon the statistics examined and the assumptions made in the above statements. There are two schools of thought about the way to position the best hitters around the setter. One way is to have the setter "lead" the middle hitter. This means that the setter comes before (serves before) the middle hitter in the rotation order. The second way is to have the setter "follow" the middle hitter. In this scenario, the middle hitter comes before the setter in the rotation order. Either one of these rotation orders shown in Figure 3-5 would be traditional possibilities for the Kennedy team, based on the statistics provided in the box score and the cumulative statistics. The advantage of know-

Figure 3-4: Kennedy Cumulative Statistics

Player	No.	GP	K	E	TA	PCT.	A	SA	SE	RE	DG	BS	BA	TB
Reed	13	9	5	1	13	0.308	0	1	2	0	2	0	2	2
Brenden	8	34	27	21	76	0.079	8	9	12	4	27	3	5	8
Franco	3	101	235	97	623	0.222	53	30	41	19	360	2	22	24
Robertson	11	102	110	42	280	0.243	1171	36	42	1	245	9	50	59
Wilson	10	44	10	4	26	0.231	135	2	14	0	41	3	10	13
Schneider	12	98	222	90	526	0.251	20	13	34	3	187	22	73	95
Macias	9	33	21	14	65	0.108	3	0	5	3	14	3	6	9
Keefe	5	104	445	170	1216	0.226	27	29	35	26	351	12	39	51
Nelson	14	14	16	4	32	0.375	4	3	4	3	21	2	0	2
Langley	4	106	236	114	604	0.202	34	46	41	26	327	9	30	39
Manderfeld	6	105	391	113	955	0.291	33	33	30	29	286	17	68	85
Totals		106	1718	670	4416	0.237	1488	202	260	127	1816	82	305	387

Figure 3-5: Possible Rotation Orders for Kennedy

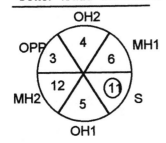

Rotation Order if the Setter "leads" the Middle

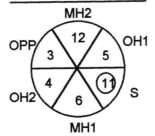

Rotation Order if the Setter "follows" the Middle

ing the opponent's rotation order is that this knowledge will help the coach to match up the line-up in such a way that the team would be provided an advantage. (Match-ups will be discussed at length in Chapter 5.)

Further, the coach can glean even more information from the box score and the cumulative statistics. The following information may help the coach plan some tactical strategy for future matches against Kennedy. Obviously, it would be better actually to see the future opponents play, but that may not be possible.

• Expect Keefe and Manderfeld to get set when they are in the front row—they are Kennedy's most frequently set players.

• Langley appears to be one of Kennedy's weakest hitters (.202 hitting efficiency).

• Kennedy's middle blockers (No. 6 and No. 12) are strong—try to set the ball away from them or make them move to block.

• Kennedy's opposite (No. 3), their setter (No. 11) and their outside hitters (Nos. 4 and 5) appear to be much weaker blockers—try to set the ball in their areas.

• It appears that they receive serve with three or four players (Nos. 3, 4, 5 and 6) because their reception errors are fairly balanced. Other players have too few errors to receive the serve consistently.

• Manderfeld (No. 6) has the most reception errors—serve toward her area.

• Robertson (No. 11) has the most service aces—be ready for her serve.

• It appears that they predominantly use six players because of the number of games played by the other players.

Box Score Accuracy Check
Aces vs. Reception Errors

One team's total service aces should equal the other team's total reception errors. Remember, team reception errors count toward the total reception errors. For example, if North has 10 service aces, then South should have a total of 10 reception errors, two of which may be team errors.

Assists vs. Kills

Team A's total assists should be nearly equal to–but never more than–its kills. The difference would be due to overpasses by Team B, which were subsequently attacked for a kill by Team A. It is possible but unlikely that a team's assists and kills would be equal.

Total Team Blocks vs. Hitting Errors

One team's total team blocks should not exceed the other team's hitting errors.

Individual Blocks vs. Team Blocks

The individual blocks total is determined by counting one point for each block solo and one point for each block assist. The total team blocks tally is figured by awarding one point for a block solo and one-half point for a block assist.

Attacks and Digs

One team's attack total should be nearly equal to its own kills + errors + the other team's digs. For example, if Team A had 46 kills and 14 errors and Team B had 40 digs, the total would be 100—this should be close to the total number of attack attempts for Team A. Conversely, say Team A knew it had 100 attack attempts with 46 kills and 14 errors. If Team B were reporting 60 digs for the match, someone has definitely miscounted or fabricated the dig totals!

Summary

• Promotion is an important part of coaching. One of the best ways to promote interest in your team and increase the knowledge of the media and fans is to provide statistics after the match.

• The Official Box Score is primarily intended to be a tool used by the media for reporting highlights about the match. In essence, the box score reports all rally ending plays (e.g., kills, blocks, aces, etc.)

in a match and additionally gives statistics about digs and assists.

•The first step to completing the box score is to record the events of the match on the AVCA Worksheet. After the match the totals from the worksheet are transferred to the box score.

•The abbreviated or short box score can be used by the media when it is not possible to reproduce the entire Official Box Score. The short box score lists all rally ending plays by individual players (e.g., kills, aces and blocks).

•Although the box score is primarily a media tool, the information in the box score can be used to draft a rough scouting report on an upcoming opponent if the coach has not seen the opponent play.

Chapter 4

"For most people the activity portion of life is overemphasized at the expense of the rest phase. Don't suffer from picnic deficiency!"

Deepak Chopra, writer and healer

Points Per Rotation Statistics

Rarely does a season pass without a team encountering some kind of slump or decline in performance. A coach always hopes that this condition is a temporary situation which will disappear as suddenly as it occurred. However, sometimes the slump starts the first day of competition! As a result, the diagnosis of a team's weaknesses and deficiencies is one of the coach's primary responsibilities. The challenge, then, is to find a cure. One of the most valuable tools available to the coach for pinpointing the source of the problem can be the official score sheet. Do not leave the gym without it. Many schools are now using "self-carbon" score sheets (NCR™ forms) so that each school can have a copy. From the information on the score sheet, the coach can calculate the points per rotation for his/her own team and the opponents. Since the game of volleyball is played in parts–rotation by rotation–it is logical to look for a tool to dissect the rotations. This statistic can help the coach to diagnose many of the problems a team may be having within the rotation order.

Computing Options

The rating system used to calculate points per rotation is the normal scoring process used on the score sheet. There is no need for the coach to use any other form or method to gather the data for computing the points per rotation statistic. The official score sheet is a ready-made tool for the coach; as a result, the official scorekeeper has unknowingly become a member of the coach's statistics crew!

The points per rotation statistic yields the average number of points scored in each rotation. A rotation is defined as one player's term of service. A player may serve once or several times in each rotation. If his/her team scores a point, the same player serves again and continues to do so until the opponents score a side-out. The side-out ends the server's term of service. During a game, a single player may have any number of terms of service. The longer the game the more rotations will occur, thereby resulting in more terms of service for each player. Use the following formula to calculate points per rotation for an individual rotation. The

overall team points per rotation is routinely called "points for" or "points scored." The points per rotation for the opponents is commonly referred to as the "points scored against."

> computing points per rotation
> total number of points scored/number of rotations = points per rotation (PPR)

Figure 4-1 shows an example of an official score sheet from one game of a match. It shows the points per rotation calculations for each rotation and the overall (average) team points per rotation for a single game. The sample score sheet shown is for collegiate women. Methods for keeping the official score vary for high school or open competition, but the same calculations can be gleaned from the information recorded on any score sheet.

For example, in Figure 4-1, South's No. 9 was the second player to serve on the team. She served the first time and scored her team's second point. She served again, but Central gained a side-out (R). This ends No. 9's term of service. She served two times and scored one

Figure 4-1: Sample Score Sheet

Points Per Rotation

Ser. Order	Player Number	SOUTH	X First Serve			Player Number	CENTRAL
1	4	①Ⓡ S 10/8 ④⑤⑥Ⓡ (4/2 = 2.0)	1̸ 2̸ 3̸	1̸ 2̸ 3̸	1	16	Ⓡ S 2/10 ⑩Sx11/2 ⑪Sx 7/13 S6/11 ⑫⑬Sx11/5 Ⓡ (4/1 = 4.0)
2	9	②Ⓡ⑦⑧⑨Ⓡ (4/2 = 2.0)	4̸ 5̸ 6̸	4̸ 5̸ 6̸	2	1̸1̸ 8̸ 11	①②ⓇⓇ (2/2 = 1.0)
3	1̸3̸ 7	③Ⓡ (1/1 = 1.0)	7̸ 8̸ 9̸	7̸ 8̸ 9̸	3	3c	③④Ⓡ S1/4 ⑭Sx5/11 ⑮ (4/2 = 2.0)
4	1̸0̸ 8̸ 10	S8/10 Ⓡ (0/1 = 0)	10 11 12	10 1̸1̸ 1̸2̸	4	9̸ 1̸0̸ 2	S10/9 ⑤⑥⑦Ⓡ (3/1 = 3.0)
5	14c	Ⓡ (0/1 = 0)	13 14 15	1̸3̸ 1̸4̸ 1̸5̸	5	12	⑧Ⓡ (1/1 = 1.0)
6	5̸ 1̸1̸ 2̸ 1̸1̸ 5	Sx4/1 S2/11 Ⓡ (0/1 = 0)	16 17	16 17	6	1̸ 4̸ 1	⑨Sx11/5 Ⓡ (1/1 = 1.0)

| South: (9/8 = 1.13) | | Code: | Served ◯ | Point ③ | Rotate Ⓡ | No Serve ☐ | Play-over Ⓟ | | Central: (15/8 = 1.85) |

S = substitution serving team   Sx = substitution receiving team

point in this rotation. The next player to serve on the South team is No. 13. Her serve begins a new rotation (term of service). Later in the game, the serve returns to No. 9; she scores the team's seventh, eighth and ninth points before Central gains a side-out. In that specific term of service (rotation), No. 9 scored three points. Therefore, No. 9 scored a total of four points in two rotations for an average of 2.0 points per rotation (4/2 = 2.0 PPR).

At the end of the game, the points per rotation can be calculated for both the individual and the team. To arrive at the individual points per rotation, tally the total points scored by an individual or substitute, then divide by the number of rotations. To determine the team's average points per rotation for the game, count the total points scored in the game and divide by the total number of rotations. The South team on the sample score sheet scored nine points and had eight rotations, which equals a game points per rotation of 1.13 (9/8 = 1.13 PPR). Central averaged 1.85 points per rotation.

Reporting Options

Points per Rotation Summary Form - Appendix, Form 17

This form displays the information gleaned from the official score sheet and provides space for the calculations of individual, game and match points per rotation. It also gives information about the net number of points a team wins or loses by rotation. If a team scores more points in a specific rotation than it gives up to the opponents, then the team has a positive net. If a team gives up more points in a rotation than it scores, the result is a negative net.

Naming the Rotations

Since it is common for a team to start with a different server in some games, it is necessary to name the rotations to facilitate meaningful game-to-game comparisons of one rotation to another. The universally accepted system for naming the rotations is based on the position of the setter within the rotation. If you have more than one setter in the line-up, pick one to use as your indicator. From this point, there are two commonly used methods of determining the rotation number a team is in at any specific time. It seems that coaches across the nation have not been able to agree on which method to use. The important thing is to select

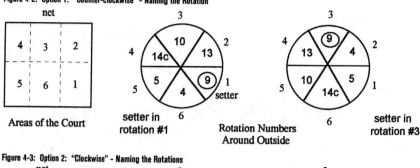

Figure 4-2: Option 1: "Counter-clockwise" - Naming the Rotation

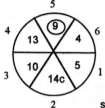

Figure 4-3: Option 2: "Clockwise" - Naming the Rotations

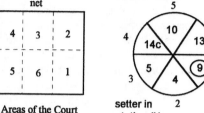

one method and stick with it so that your team understands what is meant when the coach says, "Start in rotation No. 3."

Figure 4-2 shows the first option used to name the rotations. It can be called the "counter-clockwise" method because the numbers go in the opposite direction of the rotation order. (Teams rotate clockwise.) The rotation order for the South team is used in the example. You have probably heard coaches refer to "areas" of the court when talking to servers about where they should aim their serves. These areas correspond to the numbered positions on the court. Area 1 is the same as position 1 (right back); area 2 is the same as position 2 (right front); and so on through the six positions. Imagine that the net is at the top of the page so that rotation No. 4 is left front, rotation No. 3 is center front and rotation No. 2 is right front with the server in rotation No. 1. With this option, Rotation 1 is defined as the rotation where the setter is in right back (position 1). Rotation No. 2 would be when the setter is in right front; rotation No. 3 would be when the setter is in center front (position No. 3); rotation No. 5 would find your setter in left back (position No. 5); and so on.

The second option—and probably the more common way of naming the rotations—can be called the "clockwise" method. With this naming scheme, the setter's position follows the rotation order in a clockwise rotation. Figure 4-3 diagrams this option, whereby the rotation numbers are opposite the numbers used for the areas of the court. The setter

in the right back position is still rotation No. 1, but as the setter rotates to middle back, she moves to rotation No. 2. The setter in the left back position is rotation No. 3; the setter in the center front position is rotation No. 5; and so on. Think of this method as following the rotation order (e.g., if the setter is in No. 5, then there are five rotations before she serves again). The remainder of the examples and discussion about rotations will use this method for reference to the rotations.

Starting Rotation

Figure 4-4 shows the starting rotations for the South and Central teams as taken from the sample score sheet discussed earlier. Note that the South setter, No. 9, starts in rotation No. 6. So, when recording the points per rotation statistics for rotation No. 6, the statistician knows that the setter was in right front and player No. 4 was serving for the South team. As they rotate to serve the second time, the setter will serve in rotation No. 1. The third server will be No. 13. When No. 13 serves the team will be in rotation No. 2 because the setter is in center back. When the South points per rotation sta-

Figure 4-4: Starting Line-ups for South and Central

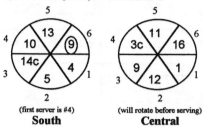

(first server is #4)
South

(will rotate before serving)
Central

tistics are compared to the points per rotation for the Central team, the South statistics are merely matched to the corresponding rotation for the Central team. In other words, it does not matter where the Central setter is located. In the example below, when player No. 9 is serving in rotation No. 1, her points per rotation would be compared to the person serving for the South team (player No. 11). If the statistician were taking statistics for the Central team, the position of the setter would indicate the rotations and the position of the setter for South would not matter.

Transferring the Data

Figure 4-5 (see page 38) shows the PPR summary for the match between South and Central. The official score sheet from game No. 1 is shown in Figure 4-1. The top of the points per rotation form (PPR) has six wheels or circles divided into six wedges representing each of the six rotations. There is one double circle for each of the five possible games of the match and one double circle for the match totals. In the points per rotation summary sheet, the inner circle (shaded) is used to record the opponent's points scored in each rotation. The outer circle is used to record your team's points scored in each rotation.

To transfer information from the score sheet (Figure 4-1) to the PPR form (Figure 4-5), follow the steps outlined below. Keep in mind that the South setter is player No. 9 and the South team started the first game in rotation No. 6.

First, from the score sheet, transfer the total points scored in each rotation by each respective team. These are recorded in the double circles for each game at the top of the summary form. Record the points scored by your team for each rotation in the outer circle and the points scored by the opponents for each rotation in the inner shaded circle. Be sure to record them in the appropriate wedge based upon the rotation number. In game No. 1, the first server was No. 4 for South—the team started in rotation No. 6. South scored four points during her two terms of service. A "4" is entered on the outer circle for rotation No. 6. The Central team scored four points in the same rotation. A "4" is entered on the inner circle for rotation No. 6. The second server for South was the setter (No. 9) in rotation No. 1 and she scored four

points during her two terms of service. Enter a "4" in the outer circle for rotation No. 1. Central scored two points in the same rotation, so a "2" is entered on the inner circle in rotation No. 1. Essentially, the information in the circles will tell the coach how many points his/her team scored vs. the number of points which were scored against them in each rotation.

Next, transfer the points per rotation statistics already calculated from the score sheet (Figure 4-1) onto the center section on the summary form for points per rotation. Some coaches may not feel they need the middle section with the "points per rotation." It is used to record their PPR and the PPR for the opponents and has an area to record the number of rotations (terms of service). This information can be a permanent record for the coach without having to refer back to the score sheets each time. Now list your team averages, a slash and then the opponent's averages for each rotation in each game. If you wish, you can transfer only your team averages. Record the number of rotations used for your team in the "# of Rot." column after the average. The South team has an average of 2.0 PPR in rotation No. 1, while the central team has an average of 1.0 PPR. This means the South team scores an average of two points each time No. 9 serves. The Central team scores an average of one point against this rotation.

Complete the "match total" double circle by adding all of the points scored in each specific rotation during the match. If five games were played, you would add together all of the points scored in rotation No. 1 during each game and record the total in the appropriate wedge for rotation No. 1. Record your team total in the outer circle and the opponent total in the shaded inner circle. For example, South scored a total of 21 points through five games while they were in rotation No. 1. Central scored a total of five points in the same rotation.

To complete the "net score by rotation" at the bottom, subtract the points your team scored in each rotation from the points the opponent scored in each rotation. For example, in game No. 1, rotation No. 1, the South team scored four points and the Central team scored two points. The net score for the South team is a plus two (+2). This net score is recorded under rotation No. 1, game No. 1, on the bottom of the summary form.

Do the same for all rotations in all games.

Finally, complete the "match totals" section for the net score. Subtract all of the points scored for your team in each rotation from the points scored by the opponents. This will give you the overall picture of how the team scored in the match, rotation by rotation.

Interpreting the Data

Since the points per rotation statistic yields the average number of points scored in each rotation, it gives the coach information about several combinations of factors. A cursory examination of the score sheets will reveal which rotations produce the most points and which rotations result in most of the opponent's points. The key to interpreting this information is to determine the most logical reason for the scoring trends. Some of the factors which influence point scoring in each rotation are:

• Effectiveness of the serve - A tougher serve increases the probability of scoring and a missed serve eliminates the opportunity.

• Ability of the serving team to block and play defense against the opponent's serve reception plays - Are there mismatches with strong hitters and weak blockers and/or is the defense positioned strategically?

• Ability of the serving team to score points in transition following a successful dig - Is the setter making good set selections in each rotation?

• Effectiveness of the serve reception - Does the passing allow the setter to choose any option, thereby forcing the opponent's defense to stretch?

• Predictability of the offense and/or the setter - Does the team have easily anticipated tendencies in side-out and point scoring situations?

Every team will display match-to-match deviations in points per rotation. A star hitter will have an off night or a jump server may have an unusually impressive night. The coach should note and address such unproductive trends continuing over a period of several matches.

Points per Rotation Summary Form

From the match totals data in Figure 4-5, the South coach could draw some specific conclusions. First, he can assume that rotation No. 1 is a very strong rotation for his team in this match against

Points Per Rotation Summary

South _____ vs Central _____ Date 10/27 Scores 9-15, 15-12, 11-15, 15-11, 15-13

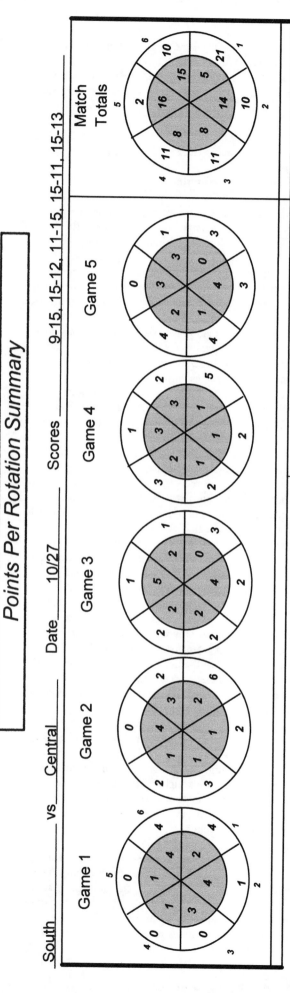

KEY: INNER CIRCLE = POINTS SCORED BY THE OPPONENTS IN EACH ROTATION
OUTER CIRCLE = POINTS SCORED BY YOUR TEAM IN EACH ROTATION

POINTS PER ROTATION = TOTAL POINTS SCORED / NUMBER OF ROTATIONS
NET SCORE BY ROTATION = POINTS YOU SCORED - POINTS SCORED BY THE OPPONENTS

(South/Central) POINTS PER ROTATION

Rotation	Game 1 / # of Rot.	Game 2 / #	Game 3 / #	Game 4 / #	Game 5 / #	Match Totals / #
1	2.0 / 1.0 2	3.0 / 1.0 2	1.0 / 0 3	1.7 / .3 3	1.0 / 0 3	1.6 / .4 13
2	1.0 / 2.0 1	1.0 / .5 2	.7 / 1.3 3	1.0 / .5 2	1.5 / 2.0 2	.9 / 1.3 11
3	0 / 3.0 1	1.5 / .5 2	1.0 / 1.0 2	1.0 / .5 2	2.0 / .5 2	1.0 / .7 11
4	0 / 1.0 1	1.0 / .5 2	1.0 / 1.0 2	1.5 / 1.0 2	2.0 / 1.0 2	1.2 / .9 9
5	0 / 1.0 1	0 / 2.0 2	.5 / 2.5 2	.5 / 1.5 2	0 / 1.5 2	.2 / 1.8 9
6	2.0 / 4.0 2	1.0 / 1.5 2	.5 / 1.0 2	1.0 / 1.5 2	.5 / 1.5 2	1.1 / 1.7 9

NET SCORE BY ROTATION

Rotation	Game 1	Game 2	Game 3	Game 4	Game 5	Match Totals
1	+2	+4	+3	+4	+3	+16
2	-3	+1	-2	+1	-1	-4
3	-3	+2	0	+1	+3	+3
4	-1	+1	0	+1	+2	+3
5	-1	-4	-4	-2	-3	-14
6	0	-1	-1	-1	-2	-5

Central. His team scored 21 points and gave up only five points in this rotation for a +16 net. Secondly, he has cause to be concerned about rotation No. 5. In rotation No. 5, the South team has a negative net of 14, scoring only two points and giving up a total of 16 points. The -14 net is not acceptable if it is a pattern over the course of many matches. South's problem here seems to be that it is not scoring enough points and the players are also allowing the opponents to score too many points. This could be a match-up problem in the front row; it could be a problem with the setter's set selection; or it could be a problem with the server in that rotation. The coach would need to examine the attack charts, set selection chart and the serving statistics closely to determine which scenario was most likely. Discovering the root of the problem can take some good detective work! It is also important to check statistics from past matches to see if this is a consistent problem. Hopefully, it is only a one-match anomaly. Generally, a discrepancy of a plus or minus five points in a five-game match is not significant. This would only be one point per game. In Figure 4-5, the rotations other than Nos. 1 and 5 fall within acceptable ranges.

Diagnosing Problems

•Situation 1: Early in the season, a coach realizes that her collegiate team, Southwest, is developing a troubling trend of being "slow starters" in games. Up until this point, Southwest's coach has been using the same starting line-up with the same first server. Invariably, it takes Southwest several rotations before it seems to get on track. The team does well for awhile, but later there is another dip in performance. She has discussed this tendency with the team members and has asked them to set goals to "come out ready to play." Midway through the season, this trend has continued, despite all of her words. It is time to look for other solutions. There may be many different reasons for Southwest's sporadic performance. One of the first things the coach should evaluate is the rotation order and/ or the service order. An easy explanation for this tendency might be detected by examining the points per rotation ratios.

Figure 4-6 shows the points per rotation statistics for the Southwest team. Remember, the rotation number will tell what position the setter occupies at that

Figure 4-6: Southwest Rotation Statistics

net

Service Order	Rotation Number	PPR
1. #14 (OH1)	Rotation 6 (setter in RF)	0.5
2. #9 (S)	Rotation 1 (setter in RB)	0.4
3. #10 (MH1)	Rotation 2 (setter in CB)	0.3
4. #6 (OH2)	Rotation 3 (setter in LB)	1.1
5. #13 (OPP)	Rotation 4 (setter in LF)	1.2
6. #2 (MH2)	Rotation 5 (setter in CF)	0.9

exact moment. The rotation order tells the serving order of the team. For example, Southwest has a serving order where the first server is the outside hitter (No. 14) and the setter starts in right front. Southwest starts the game in rotation No. 6. After several weeks, Southwest's points per rotation ratios (with the same rotation order) were very interesting (see Figure 4-6).

Southwest's coach would be wise to change the service order, based on the above statistics. Notice that the first three servers (Nos. 14, 9 and 10) have the lowest points per rotation ratio (0.5, 0.4, and 0.3). This reflects the trend the coach is seeing, whereby the team gets off to a slow start in every game. The points per rotation ratios do not tell you why this is happening, only that it is. Maybe the reason is poor serving, poor blocking or poor defense—it could be any number of things. The points per rotation ratios also tell that the next three servers (Nos. 6, 13 and 2) and/or rotations (rotation Nos. 4, 5 and 6) are much more productive. Their points per rotation ratios are 1.1, 1.2 and 0.9. This means that Southwest is scoring more points in rotation Nos. 3, 4 and 5. Southwest's coach should consider changing the service order by starting in rotation No. 3 and having No. 6 as the first server. Figure 4-7 shows the new change.

By rotating the service order three spots ahead (in volleyball lingo, this is "turning or spinning the wheel"), the coach has managed to have the three most productive rotations first. Rather than starting the game with player No. 14 serving in rotation No. 6, Southwest is now starting with player No. 6 serving in rotation No. 3. The least productive rotation and/or server is now last instead of third. This is a minor coaching adjustment

Figure 4-7: Southwest New Service Order

net

Service Order	Rotation Number	PPR
1. #6 (OH2)	Rotation 3 (setter in LB)	1.1
2. #13 (OPP)	Rotation 4 (setter in LF)	1.2
3. #2 (MH2)	Rotation 5 (setter in CF)	0.9
4. #14 (OH1)	Rotation 6 (setter in RF)	0.5
5. #9 (S)	Rotation 1 (setter in RB)	0.4
6. #10 (MH1)	Rotation 2 (setter in CB)	0.3

which could make a significant improvement in the scoring for Southwest. The next job for Southwest's coach is to look further at these weak rotations to determine reasons for the low ratios. Correcting the low points per rotation ratios might take longer, but in the meantime, this service order adjustment has helped the team. Coaches should, however, be cautioned about making these types of adjustments without the cumulative statistics from many matches.

•Situation 2: You are the head coach of the East High School team. Your team is having problems scoring points during matches and is losing games by very close scores (e.g., 15-13). To check this assumption, you can calculate your team's overall PPR by adding all of the points scored and dividing by the total number of rotations. If you do the same for the opponents you will arrive at the rate the opponents score against your team. Figure 4-8 shows an example of how to calculate total points per rotation for a team.

Figure 4-8: Total Points Per Rotation

	Total Points Scored	Total Rotations	Total PPR
East:	125	168	0.74
Opponents:	154	168	0.92
Opponent's points scored = "points against"			

As you review the team's statistics, you find that your team has an overall PPR of 0.74, while allowing a PPR "against" (what you are allowing the opponents to score) of 0.92. These averages are considered low for normal high school teams. But, even though your team is holding the opponents to a low points per rotation ratio (0.92), it concerns you that your own team is scoring at an even less efficient rate (0.74). On a brighter note, for a high school team, you have a better than average team passing efficiency of 2.0. These statistics tell you that your team is doing a good job of serve reception and siding out because you are holding the opponent's PPR relatively low. However, your low PPR indicates that when you are serving, your team is not scoring at a very efficient rate–or at least not scoring enough points to win. To diagnose the cause of this specific problem, you would want to consider the following factors:

•Weak serving - Check your serving efficiency. When a team is not scoring, the first thing the coach should look at is the effectiveness of the serve (e.g., too many errors; poor placement; lollipop serves).

•Poor blocking and/or poor defense - Perhaps this indicates a need to change the defense. If the serve efficiency is within normal ranges, then the coach should check the team defense and blocking (e.g., weak and ineffective blocking; blocking mismatches or one exceptionally poor blocker; type of defensive coverage; lack of defensive effort and/or skill).

•Less than effective transition offense - This occurs when the coach's own team is serving. If the team blocking and defense seem acceptable, then the coach should look for reasons the team is not scoring points in transition offense after a successful dig (e.g., set and/or play selection; hitter's shot selection or judgment).

What Are Normal Points per Rotation Ratios?

In general, the higher the level of play, the more rotations it will take to score points. Evenly matched teams also produce longer games and therefore more rotations to score points. As a general rule, longer games result in more rotations and lower points per rotation values. At the conclusion of a very one-sided match, the points per rotation will be heavily skewed to the winning team. Jim Coleman has provided statistical ranges for various levels of play. The following values reflect normal points per rotation (PPR) ratios for a game.

High School/"B" Open	12-16 rotations @ 1.0-1.4 PPR
Collegiate/"AA" Open	18-22 rotations @ .7-.9 PPR
International Women/	
"AAA" Open	24-28 rotations @.5-.6 PPR
International Men	28-32 rotations @ .4-.5 PPR

Summary

•The points per rotation statistic yields the average number of points scored in each rotation. A rotation is defined as one player's term of service.

•The official score sheet is a ready made tool for the coach. It will provide all of the information necessary to calculate points per rotation statistics. Be sure to get a copy of the score sheet before leaving the gym.

•At the end of the game, the points per rotation can be calculated for both the individual and the team. To arrive at the individual points per rotation, tally the total points scored by an individual or substitute, then divide by the number of rotations. To determine the team's average points per rotation for the game, count the total points scored in the game and divide by the total number of rotations.

•Since it is common for a team to start with a different server in some games, it is necessary to name the rotations to facilitate meaningful game-to-game comparisons of one rotation to another. The universally accepted system of naming the rotations is based on the position of the setter within the rotation. If you have more than one setter in the line-up, pick one to use as your indicator.

•The "Points per Rotation Summary" is ideal for recording all important information regarding PPR statistics. Once completed, it presents the coach with a valuable tool for diagnosing problems relative to points scored and points scored against. The key to interpreting the data is to find the most logical reason for the scoring trends.

•Minor changes in the rotation order (service order) can be effective in solving some team scoring problems.

Chapter 5

"If the only tool you have is a hammer, you tend to see every problem as a nail." Abraham Maslow, psychologist

Basics of Charting and Scouting

Of course, utilizing videotape is the best way to record the sequence and exact events of a match. However, absent a video recording, "charting" is the next best way to record the hitting tendencies, offense, defense and other subtleties of a specific team. Almost every coach and avid volleyball fan has developed a system for charting a game. Some coaches like to record the major areas of play like offense, defense and serve reception to prepare for an upcoming match with an opponent. These coaches may use separate charts to record keys to the opponent's tendencies. Other coaches prefer to get a sense of the flow of the action by charting as much of the match on one form as possible. Fans of the game may have developed a system of recording the events of the match with a style of charting which is a combination of many systems. The information here is not necessarily the only way to scout and chart, but it provides some standardized methods for the novice. Hopefully, more seasoned veterans will also find some valuable insights.

Just as there are many different methods of charting a game, there are also many reasons for charting. The media and fans use charting to pass along information about the match to others. Today, it is possible to get some very detailed descriptions–and even real-time broadcasts–of a match on the internet. Charts are also used to discuss the flow of the match and possibly to do some "armchair coaching." Some spectators find it much easier to follow and analyze the match when they are doing some type of chart. Coaches use charting to learn more about their team and to scout other team's tactics. Even when videotape is available, most coaches break the tape down into some form of written analysis. Also, having a videotape allows one to work at a slower pace. Initially, while recording statistics during a match, it is difficult to keep up with the speed of play. Gradually,

charting skills will improve. It is amazing how much information can be recorded during play. Get your players to try it. Coaches will be surprised how much more players pay attention to a match and how much more they take away as opposed to just sitting and watching.

This chapter is designed to present common systems for recording events during a match. These systems can be used for scouting, coaching or spectating. Previous chapters have detailed types of statistical analysis and methods for calculating game averages. This chapter will explain the variety of information which can be recorded, how it is useful and efficient methods for recording. Each individual can select the recording techniques which best meet the needs of the team. Another purpose of this chapter is to standardize the language and format used for charting in the United States. (The terminology used is taken directly from USA Volleyball educational information.) Jim Coleman is responsible for developing the concepts for most of the information. (Chapter 7 is an advanced tutorial on charting.)

Understanding the Basics
Getting a Good View

Whenever possible, find a spot behind the endline to view a match. This vantage point allows the viewer to have the best angle from which to watch the action on the court—especially the action at the net. The movement of the offense, set delivery, blockers and defense are all easier to see from the endline than from the sideline. In many ways, coaches on the bench have one of the worst seats in the gym! When scouting a specific team, it is helpful to sit directly behind the team. Videotaping should also be done from an elevated position behind the court. A sideline view often distorts the action or requires the camera to be moved back and forth, resulting in views which do not include the entire court. Many teams have constructed elevated platforms behind the court specifically for videotaping. The platform should be high enough to see the team easily on the other side of the net.

Hitting and Setting Terminology

Some basic knowledge of setting and hitting terminology is necessary to do a

Figure 5-1: Set Terminology

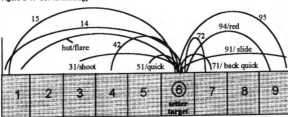

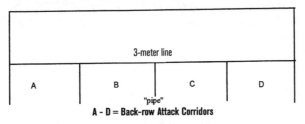

3-meter line

A   B   C   D

"pipe"

A - D = Back-row Attack Corridors

The first number indicates the area of the net where the set falls.
The second number indicates the height of the set above the net.
Back-row set height depends on the quickness of the offense and the jumping ability of the hitter.

1st tempo = quick set (1)
e.g., 51, 71, 91

2nd tempo = 2 set
e.g., 42, 72, cross, tandem

3rd tempo = high set (4 or 5)
e.g., 15, 94

Typical Play (Cross):
Outside hitter hits "14"
Middle hits "51" (quick)
Opposite hits "42" (cross)
Back-row hits "D"

Figure 5-2: Other Typical Plays

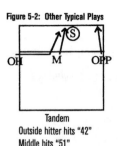

Tandem
Outside hitter hits "42"
Middle hits "51"
Opposite hits "94"

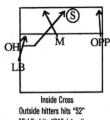

Inside Cross
Outside hitters hits "52"
Middle hits "31" (shoot)
Opposite hits "94"
Back-row hits "A"

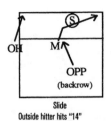

Slide
Outside hitter hits "14"
Middle hits "92" (slide)
Back-row hits "B-C" (pipe)
Setter can attack on second ball

good job of charting and/or scouting. Figure 5-1 (page 43) diagrams the types of sets and gives common terminology for each. Also listed are some common volleyball slang terms for different sets. Teams will develop their own pet names for plays and sets within their offensive systems. However, if the sport of volleyball is to continue to grow, it is important that coaches speak a common language. This system of numbering sets and areas of the net was developed by Jim Coleman and has been adopted in this country by USA Volleyball. The system is also used internationally. Coleman's system allows coaches and players to give a specific height and location for a set.

At one time, setters were the only players on the court who "called" the team's plays—usually before the ball was served. Now it is also common for the hitters to call for a specific set as the pass is being delivered to the setter's target area (see Figure 5-2). Most teams also have some sort of hand signal system for calling plays in situations where the crowd noise can impede verbal communication.

For purposes of describing the location of a set, the net is divided into nine equal sections (1 meter each) along its length from antenna to antenna. These areas are numbered from 1 to 9. Facing the net, the areas move along the net from left to right. So, area 1 starts at the left antenna and area 9 ends at the right antenna. The height of the set is described by a numbering system which tells the hitter how high above the net the set will travel. Obviously, this information is important for the timing and direction of the hitter's approach. With these two numbers, the hitter will know where the set will fall along the length of the net, as well as the height of the set (the first number called indicates the area of the net and the second number called indicates the height). For example, a "52" set means that the set will be delivered to area 5 of the net and it will be 2 to 4 feet above the

height of the net. A "71" is a set to area 7 and will be only 1 to 2 feet high. Sets numbered "4" are medium height and a "5" set is considered a very high set. In the women's game, a "slide" is a common name for a fast back-set whereby the hitter approaches along the net and makes a one-footed take-off. This type of approach is less common in the men's game. A slide could be a "71", "81", "91" or a second-tempo (e.g., 92) set to any of these three areas behind the setter.

Serve Reception Offense vs. Transition Offense

Serve reception offense and side-out offense are interchangeable terms used for describing a team's first play of the ball directly off serve reception (e.g., the serve, the pass, set and attack). Transition offense is the term originally used to describe the offensive play in point scoring opportunities (when your team serves). However, attacks which occur during rallies as the team transitions from defense to offense are also considered transition offense, even though a kill may score a side-out rather than a point. Basically, any attack which occurs after the initial attack off the serve reception is now routinely considered transition offense. Knowing how well your team executes the offensive system when receiving the serve and during transition is critical. (This concept will be discussed later in the section on interpreting data.)

As coaches become more adept at taking statistics, separate charts will be kept which give serve reception and transition offense information. A common way to separate serve reception offense from transition offense is to keep an attack chart which shows two or more courts for each rotation. On one of the courts, diagram what happened on only the initial play (attack) off each serve reception and on the second chart, diagram all of the other attacks which occur after the initial attack.

Kills for Points vs. Kills for Side-Out

Information about the number of kills scored for points as opposed to kills scored for side-outs is not commonly kept by most domestic volleyball teams. International teams, however, classify and report kill statistics in two categories—either the kill scores a point or it scores a side-out. This method is a slightly different way of looking at side-out offense vs. transition offense. A chart or computer program which shows when the kills occurred will give this data. Normally, a team will score about three times more kills for side-out than it scores for points. During the 1996 Olympics, for example, the top four women's teams averaged 29 percent of their kills for points and 71 percent of their kills for side-outs. If the ratio of kills for points vs. kills for side-outs is significantly different than this 1:3 ratio, the coach may want to find out what is actually happening in each rotation. Looking at the points per rotation (Chapter 4) will give information regarding whether your team is having trouble scoring or is giving up too many points. Of course, the best scenario would be that your team is scoring easily and not giving up many points—if this is the case, who cares about the ratio of kills for points vs. kills for side-out!

The Basics of Defensive Systems

There are many types of defensive systems used in volleyball. A basic knowledge of these systems for "floor defense" is necessary to chart or diagram a team's defense properly. Floor defense is the term routinely used to describe the positioning of the non-blocking members of the defensive team on the court. Teams usually switch positions after the serve to play one assigned front-row position (e.g., middle blocker/hitter), and then when in the back row, switch to play one assigned back-row position (e.g., left back). To this end, the person charting will normally see a lot of switching of positions after the ball is served. The examples of defensive positioning used here assume a double block is used and the set is delivered to the opposing team's left-side attacker. Figure 5-3 shows the basic positioning of the defensive players in several common defenses. Most teams will use a combination of more than one defensive system or use several different defenses to stop specific players. The most important thing in charting defenses is to rec-

Figure 5-3: Common Defensive Systems

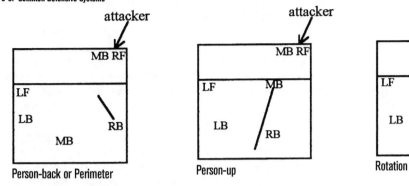

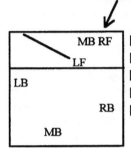

Person-cross

Perimeter = all non blockers drop back to dig; LF and RB "read and release" for tips.

Person-up = middle back moves up and follows behind the blockers along the 3-meter line to dig tips; all non blockers dig deep.

Rotation = defender behind block "rotates" up for tips; all other non blockers dig deep.

Person-cross = front-row non blocker moves across to cover tips; all others dig deep.

ognize how teams set up to defend against individual plays or players. The coach needs to communicate to the team what options may successfully result in a kill against a set defense. For example, a team may use a rotation defense to defend against an opponent's outside hitters and a perimeter defense against the opposite hitters. It is especially important to know the defensive scheme against middle attackers and combination plays (e.g., cross). Also important is the "base" defensive position—where are the defensive players stationed while the offensive play is developing (e.g., is someone ready to dig or block a dump by the setter)?

Blocking Schemes

The blocking system used by an opponent is important to know when planning a team's attack strategy. Blocking becomes both more important and more complex at higher levels of play. Rather than detail many complicated blocking systems, the points listed below give some clues for the coach to identify. Some of the key points to recognize about the opponent's blocking strategy and tactics include, but are not limited to:

• The base position of the blockers: Where do they start in relation to the hitters (wide or narrow)?

• The size and net penetration of the

blockers: Do they get over the net? Are certain blockers stronger or weaker?

• The quickness and mobility of the blockers: Can the middle cover the opposing middle hitter and still get outside to block an outside attack?

• The primary focus for the blockers: Do they watch the setter release the ball and then find the hitter or do they focus on the ball?

• The hands of the blockers: How is the block set? Does the middle close the block (no seam)? Do they give the line away? Does the outside blocker "turn the block into the court?" Does the block drift? Find the weaknesses.

• The blocking strategy and tactics for defending against back-row attacks.

• The blocking scheme used for combination plays: Who blocks first tempo attacks and who blocks second tempo attacks? Can the middle blocker get outside for a higher set when he/she has to hold and read or are outside blockers sometimes going one-on-one with the hitter?

• The scheme for blocking the middle hitter: Does the left-side blocker "help" block the quick attack? Does the middle blocker "read" the setter and jump with the release of the ball or does the blocker "commit" to the middle hitter and jump with the hitter?

• The adjustment of the blockers to the offense: Can and do the blockers change strategy or tactics during the match?

• The blocker's movement on a bad pass: Does the middle blocker release to the outside on a poor pass?

• The blocker's position on the court as the setter touches the ball: Is a dump or second-ball attack open when the setter is front-row?

Recording Options

With technical knowledge about the types of sets used–and good powers of observation–it is possible for anyone to complete an attack chart. Whether a person is scouting opponents, charting his/her own team or being an avid fan, it is relatively easy to pick up a team's hitting tendencies during a match. At the end of a match, the chart will give important information about each player's role, their effectiveness and their favorite types of sets.

Attack Chart - Appendix, Form 8

The attack chart was described at length in Chapter 2. This basic form can be used to chart all attacks by players on a team during a match. A court is provided to chart the hits of each player. It is a good tool but it does not give a coach a sense of the number and the types of sets a player received in each rotation. At higher levels of competition, it is critical for the coach to have rotational information available (see Chapter 7).

Scouting Chart - Appendix, Form 18

Whether a coach is taking data on a future opponent or sitting on the bench during a match, the scouting chart shown in Form 18 is a good tool. The scouting chart allows the coach to record both serve reception and transition offense by rotation. The set selection tendencies of the setter can be noted and counted by the number of sets delivered to each hitter. With this type of chart, the coach can see the approach patterns of all of the hitters, as well as their attack tendencies.

Figure 5-4 shows a portion of a scouting chart for one rotation. Two courts are provided for serve reception because a team will normally have more than one serve reception formation (align-

Figure 5-4: Abbreviated Scouting Chart

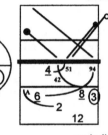

serve receive

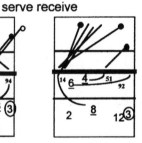

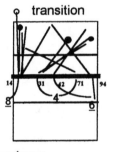

transition

Rotation 1

underlined numbers indicate front-row players

ment of players on the court) for a rotation. All of the attacks after the initial serve reception attack are recorded on the transition court. The lines from the player's base position toward the net indicate the approach pattern of the hitters. On the first serve reception court, notice Nos. 6, 2 and 8 receiving the serve in a three-person serve reception. No. 12 is hidden deep on the court and No. 4 is up close to the net. The setter is No. 3, ready to move toward the target area for a pass. The approach patterns for the attackers shows:

•No. 6 swinging to the right for a back-set (94);

•No. 4 moving to the middle for a quick attack (51);

•No. 8 moving around the middle hitter for a second tempo attack (cross/42); and

•No. 2 is moving to the left for a back-row set (A).

It is not always necessary to record

the type of set given to the attacker. This decision should be left up to the head coach.

Defense Chart - Appendix, Form 19

Preparing the gameplan for a pending opponent requires the coach to devise an offensive gameplan, within the limitations of his/her team's abilities, based on the defensive set of the opposition. The coach wants to attack the defensive weaknesses of the opponents and try to steer clear of the defensive strengths. If, for example, an opponent plays rotation defense (the player moves up behind the block), the coach should advise the team that tips behind the block will usually not be effective. The Defensive Chart can be used to highlight the strengths (e.g., strong blockers, blocking schemes) while pinpointing some tactics for exploiting the weaknesses (e.g., hit over the small setter). The chart can also be used to help the coach make decisions about match-ups. On paper, the coach should try out different rotational match-ups to determine which one offers his/her team the best advantage. Include as much or as little detail in the chart as will be helpful to the team.

An example of a completed Defensive Chart is shown in Figure 5-5. From the example, note that Southwestern is using perimeter defense for attacks by the outside hitter and rotation defense for attacks from the opposite. When the setter is front-row, Southwestern adjusts from a wide base position with the left front to a narrower base, with the left front helping to block the setter and the middle hitter. On a cross play, Southwestern moves the left front over to block the middle and the middle blocker takes the player coming around for the cross. The box in the lower right provides a quick summary of the team's blocking tendencies.

Reporting Options

The forms in this section are designed to be used for summarizing scouting data. After gathering all scouting information on the opponents, the coach can develop a gameplan and communicate this plan to the team via any one of these forms. More than one form can be used, but remember, it is possible to give the team too much information. Select the key points or highlights which the team will be able to digest and put them to use on the court. Rarely is it a wise idea to give the team all of the information at your disposal. The coach does not want the old adage, "paralysis by analysis" to become a description of his/her team's performance!

Opponent Snapshot - Appendix, Form 20

The Opponent Snapshot is a handy form for mapping out the highlights of the opponent's offensive and defensive play. Quite a bit of information can be included on the one-page form. Initially, the coach will want to use one of the other forms, probably the Scouting Chart, to take a more detailed report. Then the data can be summarized and copied onto this chart. The top of the form has an area for showing the opponent's serve reception formations in each rotation, along with the attack options for each formation. The shot charts at the bottom of the page give attackers' hitting tendencies for different sets; however, they are not meant to show every attack by every player. The center section allows for a very brief description of the opponent's offense.

Figure 5-6 (page 48) shows an example of a completed Opponent Snapshot for Walnut Grove High School. In the serve reception offense area, notice Walnut Grove uses a three-person serve reception. The coach has determined that the best passers are the outside hitters, Nos. 10 and 6, while the weakest passers are the opposite, No. 3, and one of the middles, No. 4. One can assume that the two best hitters are No. 1 (MH1) and No. 10 (OH1), because they surround the setter. The shot (attack) charts at the bottom reveal the different types of sets the hitters receive and the directional tendencies of the attacks. Looking at the shot chart for the middle hitter No. 4, it appears that all of her attacks except the "92" set are hit cross-court (power). The section for the defense shows that when Walnut Grove defends against an attack

$$\boxed{\textbf{DEFENSE CHART}}$$

Team __Southwestern__ vs. __Minnesota State__ Date __October 26__

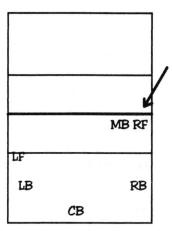

Attack from left side

Notes: Perimeter defense
MB slow to close on quick
set to outside.

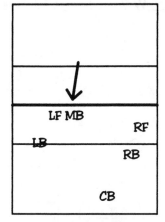

Attack from middle

Notes: Leftside helps
CB shades right, LB covers tips,
try to take power away.

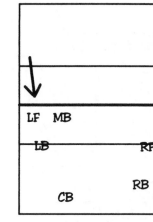

Attack from right

Notes: Rotation defense
MB does not close, CB plays seam,
leftside takes line away.

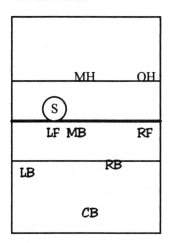

Base Position - S front row

Notes: Leftside covers
setter, RB ready for dumps.
Tip behind setter open.

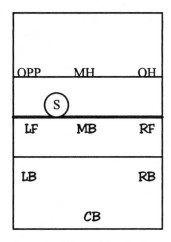

Base position - S back row

Notes: Blockers wide
LF might not close on a quick
set to MH.

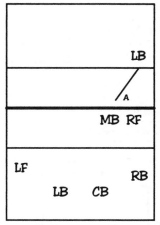

Back row attack

Notes: Use 2 blockers across
the net, non-blockers deep--hit
toward setter (RB)

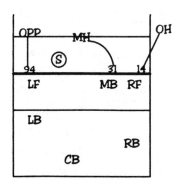

Combination plays

Notes: RF helps with 31
OPP is left one-on-one
LB stays shallow--line open

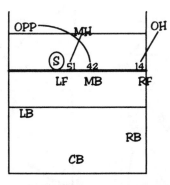

Combination plays

Notes: LF slides over to take
quick, MB takes cross, RF is
one-on-one, LB shallow

Best Blocker(s): _Opposite #9, middle #4_

Poor Blocker(s): _small setter #6_

Middle Blocker Tendencies:
good size, penetrate well if they don't
have to move, slow to close both sides

Defense vs. Slide: _LF's take one-on-one_
middles release outside

OPPONENT SNAPSHOT

Team   Walnut Grove High School

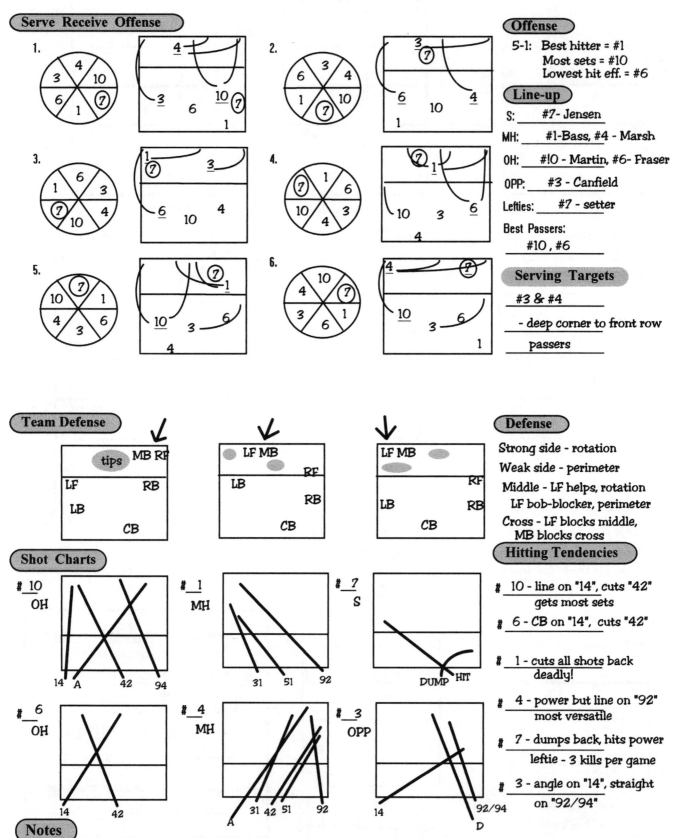

Serve Receive Offense

1.
2.
3.
4.
5.
6.

Offense

5-1:   Best hitter = #1
       Most sets = #10
       Lowest hit eff. = #6

Line-up

S: #7- Jensen

MH: #1-Bass, #4 - Marsh

OH: #10 - Martin, #6- Fraser

OPP: #3 - Canfield

Lefties: #7 - setter

Best Passers:
       #10 , #6

Serving Targets

#3 & #4

- deep corner to front row

passers

Team Defense

tips   MB RF
LF   RB
LB
       CB

LF MB
          RF
LB
          RB
       CB

LF MB
          RF
LB   RB
       CB

Defense

Strong side - rotation

Weak side - perimeter

Middle - LF helps, rotation
       LF bob-blocker, perimeter

Cross - LF blocks middle,
       MB blocks cross

Shot Charts

#_10_ OH
14   A   42   94

#_1_ MH
31   51   92

#_7_ S
DUMP HIT

#_6_ OH
14   42

#_4_ MH
A   31 42 51   92

#_3_ OPP
14   92/94
            D

Hitting Tendencies

10 - line on "14", cuts "42"
       gets most sets

6 - CB on "14", cuts "42"

1 - cuts all shots back
       deadly!

4 - power but line on "92"
       most versatile

7 - dumps back, hits power
       leftie - 3 kills per game

3 - angle on "14", straight
       on "92/94"

Notes

Hitters are predictable; setter will hit 2nd ball on good pass; tips effective; setter doesn't set front row
passers if they pass deep; setter won't go to middle on a bad pass; backrow hits are strong.

from the strong side, it plays a rotation defense. The coach has also noted that Walnut Grove appears to be vulnerable to tips inside the block.

Match-up Chart - Appendix, Form 21

In formulating a gameplan, one of the most important decisions that needs to be made is how to position the team on the court to be the most successful. This process is normally called "matching up." For example, if a coach starts her opposite in position No. 4, and the opponent starts his outside hitter in position No. 4, they will be matched up for two out of three rotations. The coach has to weigh all of the options and come to a reasonable decision. Should the strengths of his team be matched up with the strengths of the opponents or can he match-up his strengths with the opponent's weaknesses? Thought should also be given to tactical strategies—what are you going to do to attack the opponent's defense and what will you do to defend against the opponent's offense? Substitution patterns

are another consideration. Take time to plan what substitutions may be necessary during the match.

This form can be used for planning or it can be used as another type of scouting report to give the team, as many players respond well to such a visual display. Players can visualize themselves in their positions and know what to expect. The downside of the form is that the players must realize that the match-ups may change. The coach should discuss with the team the probability that match-ups will change and warn the players to be familiar with all possibilities. Practice time should be spent becoming familiar with all possible match-ups.

Figure 5-7 displays two rotations from a completed match-up chart. The opponent on this chart is Walnut Grove. Information from the Opponent Snapshot on Walnut Grove is used to complete the first two rotations. There are four courts shown for each rotation. The first (serve reception offense) court shows the serve reception offense for Walnut Grove vs. the

defense of the coach's team. Court No. 2 shows the defense of Walnut Grove vs. the serve reception offense of the coach's team. The third and fourth courts show both teams' transition offensive vs. the defense (note the comments at the bottom of the page). Find the serve reception for Walnut Grove in rotation No. 2. Notice that Walnut Grove runs a cross pattern with hitter No. 4; a slide-type set for hitter No. 3; and an outside set for hitter No. 6. The previous information on Walnut Grove tells us that No. 6 does not get many sets. So, the coach is telling the team to focus its attention on hitter Nos. 3 and 4. The coach has also indicated that the team should serve deep to the corners to force either Nos. 4 or 6 out as an option for the setter. Because No. 6 is a less threatening hitter than No. 4, it would be best for the server to serve deep to area No. 1, trying to take No. 4 out of the offense.

Game Plan - Appendix, Form 22

The Game Plan form is a written

Figure 5-7: Abbreviated Match-up Chart

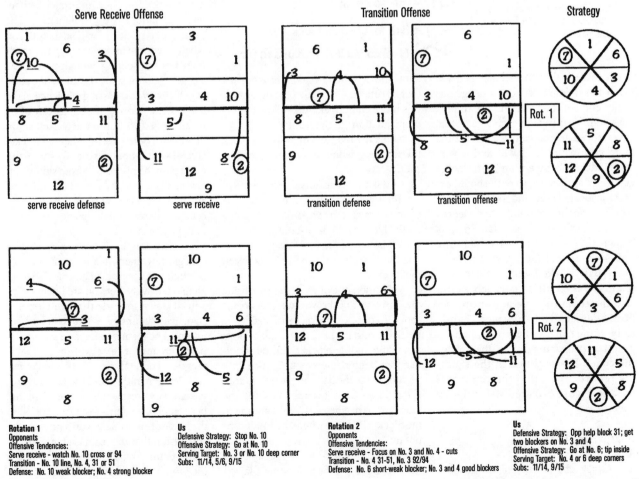

Serve Receive Offense | Transition Offense | Strategy

serve receive defense | serve receive | transition defense | transition offense | Rot. 1

Rot. 2

Rotation 1
Opponents
Offensive Tendencies:
Serve receive - watch No. 10 cross or 94
Transition - No. 10 line, No. 4, 31 or 51
Defense: No. 10 weak blocker; No. 4 strong blocker

Us
Defensive Strategy: Stop No. 10
Offensive Strategy: Go at No. 10
Serving Target: No. 3 or No. 10 deep corner
Subs: 11/14, 5/6, 9/15

Rotation 2
Opponents
Offensive Tendencies:
Serve receive - Focus on No. 3 and No. 4 - cuts
Transition - No. 4 31-51, No. 3 92/94
Defense: No. 6 short-weak blocker; No. 3 and 4 good blockers

Us
Defensive Strategy: Opp help block 31; get two blockers on No. 3 and 4
Offensive Strategy: Go at No. 6; tip inside
Serving Target: No. 4 or 6 deep corners
Subs: 11/14, 9/15

summary of what the coach has determined to be the "keys to the match." It is meant to serve as a cover sheet for other charts used to compile the scouting report. Completing the Game Plan form will help the coach to organize strategies and tactics succinctly for the team to follow. (Comments should be short and very specific.) In addition, the coach can share this information with the team and increase the potential for success. General comments like "serve tough" rarely do

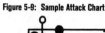

Figure 5-9: Sample Attack Chart

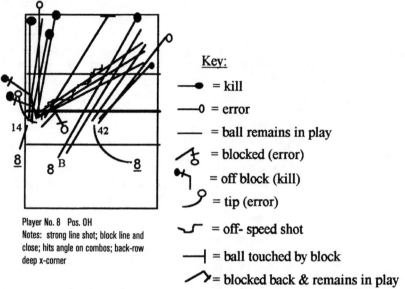

Player No. 8   Pos. OH
Notes: strong line shot; block line and close; hits angle on combos; back-row deep x-corner

Key:

= kill

= error

= ball remains in play

= blocked (error)

= off block (kill)

= tip (error)

= off- speed shot

= ball touched by block

= blocked back & remains in play

much to help the team–remember, too much information can be as dangerous as not enough information. Try to pick out one or two keys in each area. More experienced teams can usually handle more information and will find it very helpful during competition. At the collegiate level and above, a coach should expect players to learn, understand and use more information about the opponents.

A completed Game Plan Form is shown in Figure 5-8. The pending opponent is Walnut Grove, the team previously worked with in Figures 5-6 and 5-7. Ideally, the coach would like the team to have a scouting report a day or two in advance. Hopefully, some time will then be spent in practice preparing to do the things the coach has outlined in the scouting report. Note that the comments used in Figure 5-8 are brief and very specific.

Interpreting Data
Attack Charts
Attack charts can tell the coach a

great deal about the type of hitter and his/her tendencies. They can help the coach to prepare the team for a match and they can be very useful on the bench during a match to make adjustments in the defense. During a time-out or between games, players find it helpful to look at the attack charts from the opposition. A picture is worth a thousand words!

Figure 5-9 shows a sample attack chart for one player. From the chart, notice that player No. 8 has a strong line shot and a much weaker cross-court (angle) attack. A coach playing against this hitter could make the following recommendations to the team:

• Tell the blockers to move the block toward the sideline to take away the line shot.

• Make sure the outside blocker (RF) has the right hand angled back into the court to prevent the wipe-off shots going off the block and out-of-bounds.

• Make sure the block was closed so that No. 8 cannot hit the seam between the blockers.

• Position one or more diggers inside the block to dig the weaker cross-court shots. To position the digger(s) inside the block (toward the net), they should move inside the middle blocker's inside shoulder (not behind the block) and be in a position to see the ball and the hitter's arm. If the digger cannot see the ball and the hitter's arm, he/she is usually standing in the block "shadow," where the hitter cannot hit.

• Alert the back-row defense to cover the cross-court corner for this player's

back-row attack. The left back should move toward the corner.

• On combination plays, take the angle (power) shot away from this hitter (e.g., left cross or 42) by having the left front player help the middle to block and get the back-court digger to play in the seam between the two blockers.

These are examples of some simple adjustments which can be made with the information from a good attack chart. Most coaches have someone on the bench taking a similar kind of chart for their team, as well as for the opponents. A quick glance at the chart will show how effective the hitter is during the match. The fans in the stands can also become better "second guessers" of the coach if they follow the match with this kind of data!

Serve Reception Offense vs. Transition Offense
Knowing how well your team executes in serve reception and transition is important for the coach. It is even more important to know which rotations tend to be a problem for the team in each of these offensive situations. Points per rotation statistics will give information about which rotations are problematic. The points per rotation will also tell you whether your team is giving up too many points or not scoring enough points. As a coach, you must also consider the serving efficiency and passing efficiency of the team. Point scoring problems can often be attributed to unproductive transition offense. In other words, when your team is serving, it is not consistently successful at keeping the opponents from siding out. Giving up too many points can often be attributed to a lack of success in serve reception offense. Looking at every aspect of the game is critical.

• Situation 1: You are a coach of a collegiate women's team about midway through your season. The team is struggling offensively, but you are unsure why. You sit down to wade through all of the statistics at your disposal to look for a solution. The team passing and serving efficiencies appear to be within acceptable ranges. The team is one of the conference leaders in digs and the blocking totals are very respectable. Points scored per rotation are fairly balanced for all of the rotations. Finally, you come to the conclusion that the team is giving up too many points—you cannot seem to hold the opponents. This would indicate that

GAME PLAN

Team __Walnut Grove High School__   *Date* __September 27__ .

Key Players: #10 - Martin, OH---gets most of sets---hits line on strong side and angle on weak side--likes the cross on SR. (serve receive)

 #1 - Bass, MH---<u>strong, quick arm</u>--hits all shots back across her body--jump with her.

 #7 -Jensen, S---leftie who like to hit 2nd ball on good pass--3 k/g--only sets middle on good pass.

What do we need to do to win?

 Stop them on serve receive offense--they don't do as well in transition offense.

 Serve to areas where we reduce their offensive options (see serving).

 Slow down #1 and #10--be aware of where they are at all times---get our defense into their hitting angles.

 Run our offense predominantly from our weak side to attack weak blockers.

Blocking Strategy:

 Get two blockers on #1, #10 and #4 when possible--go one-on-one with the others if necessary.

 Take line away from #10--take cut-shot away from #1.

 Don't worry about the setter hitting unless the pass is perfect or very tight---take angle

 Block back row hitters with two blockers--especially #3 and #10

Serving Strategy:

 Weakest passers are #3 and #4

 When #10 receives as front row hitter, serve her deep to the corner---take her out of the offense

 In rotation 2 (#6, #3, #4 hitting) serve #4 to deep service corner

---

Attacking Strategy:

 Weak blockers #10 and #6 (outside hitters)--go at them as much as possible--spread the offense out to isolate them one-on-one---back-set a lot in transition and SR.

 Setter #7 is not a bad blocker for her size--we can hit over her---set our left side in an emergency, not the back row.

 When you run a back-set make sure the middle is running a 31 or the OPP is crossing

the first place to look further would be the side-out or serve reception offense. Using the Scouting Chart, you can look at how your team is doing in each rotation. Are you getting kills off of serve reception? You notice that one rotation seems to be a particular problem. (You may have more, but for the purposes of this example, focus on one rotation.)

Figure 5-10 shows a problem rotation from the Scouting Chart of your team. From these charts you can see that player No. 8 is not getting many sets off serve reception. Player Nos. 4 and 6 are getting a number of sets but no kills–and even worse, they are making errors which

Figure 5-10: Problem Rotation

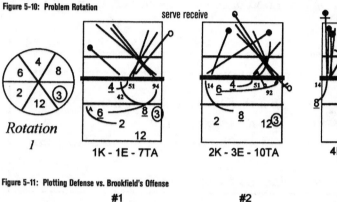

Rotation 1

1K - 1E - 7TA   2K - 3E - 10TA   4K - 0E - 12TA

Figure 5-11: Plotting Defense vs. Brookfield's Offense

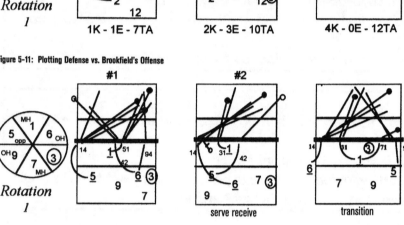

Rotation 1

#1   #2

serve receive   transition

lead directly to points for the other team. Many of your charts from other matches look much the same. The problem appears to be the set selection of the setter rather than the serve reception formation. By using the second serve reception formation and telling your setter to give No. 8 more sets, the team may be more effective, even if the passing is less efficient. The practice gym is a good place to work on a problem like this.

•Situation 2: Your high school team is getting ready to play Brookfield. You have a Scouting Chart on Brookfield from a couple of weeks ago. In practice you plan to prepare your team by practicing against the serve reception and transition plays they use. Draft some good players or use your second team to run the Brookfield offense against your starters.

The Scouting Chart can be given to the second team, asking the players to try to mimic the serve reception formations, play selection and hitting tendencies Brookfield has exhibited. (Utilize jerseys with the numbers of the Brookfield players so that the role playing is even more effective.)

The diagram in Figure 5-11 shows one of Brookfield's rotations. If you were coaching your team during a practice session before your match with Brookfield, your comments might sound something like these:

•They hit cross court - move the base positions on our block in off the line.

•Make sure our back-court diggers are positioned inside the block - CB, stay in the middle of the court.

•In serve reception No. 1 watch No. 6 - when she comes around for a 42 set our left front should yell "cross," moving in to block No. 1 while our middle blocker moves over to block No. 6.

•In serve reception No. 2 - our left front should move the base position into the middle of the court (all three blockers are in front of the setter)—be ready to block No. 5 on the 42. Our right front should watch for No. 6 swinging around to hit a 14 and help block the middle hitter on a 31.

•Set the blocks for cross-court hits - close the seams.

•Expect them to set a lot of 14s - they do not use many back-sets.

•On transition, the middle usually runs a 31 or 71—our middle needs to follow her approach as the ball is being passed. Our left front can help block the 71 and our right front can help block the 31, so start your base positions in off the sideline.

Offensive Gameplan

After preparing to face the opponent's offense, the second step in preparing a scouting plan is to make decisions about how to attack their defense. The Defense Chart will provide information to use in making these decisions. The opponent's blockers, who represent the first line of defense, should be the coach's first concern. For coaches of teams at beginning to intermediate levels of play, the blockers may not be consistent enough to present a major problem for the team. In this situation, the coach may choose to focus more on the positioning of the diggers than the tactics of the blockers. (At higher levels of play, the blocking strategies are more complex and the blocker's skills are much better. In the men's game, for example, blocking is critical. For the men, the velocity of the attack significantly reduces the probability that the floor defense can actually dig the ball. The women's game is more balanced, depending on both blocking and digging.)

Coaches should make sure that a team is able to perform an offensive gameplan. An old volleyball adage worth repeating here is that a coach should not try to do something tactically which the team cannot do technically. For example, it is a mistake for a coach to run a fast offense requiring great passing if the team has inconsistent passing skills. Therefore, select a gameplan which matches the skill level of your team.

Figure 5-12 gives one rotation from a defense chart and gives an example of some tactics which might be used offensively to score. Study the characteristics of the defensive team ("opponents") and the description of the offensive players ("us") to see if you agree with the plan. It is a very simple gameplan based on the strengths of this team and the weakness of the opponents. Each rotation should be completed in a similar manner. At one practice, the coach can lead the team through a session to practice each of the goals. Basically, the coach is trying to put her hitters into situations where they can hit with only one blocker or hit cross-

Figure 5-12: Offensive Game Plan

Us:
- good setter (No. 7) capable of consistently setting 14, 31, 42, 51 and 94
- No. 3 (OPP) can hit line or cross-court; best sets 42 and 94; average size
- No. 4 (MH) not big but quick; hits 51 and 31 well; hits angles well
- No. 10 (OH) small and quick; hits 14s cross-court; good tip placement

Opponents:
- No. 11 (OPP) good blocker; big and penetrates well
- No. 5 (MB) huge but slow moving and slow jumping
- No. 8 (OH) average size and average blocker; not exceptionally quick
- team plays rotation defense

Goal	Tactic
1. Get one-on-one blocking situations	•establish middle attack so No. 5 must commit
2. Make MB move as much as possible	•No. 4 runs 31s and then sets back-set to No. 8
	•No. 4 runs 51s and set a 14 to No. 10 - hit power
	•run 51/42 combo set a 14 to No. 10
3. Give hitters space to hit (good blockers)	•keep sets off the net (2'-4')
4. Avoid block	•No. 3 and No. 10 hit cross-court angles
	•No. 4 hit angles around middle blocker's hands
	•setter use a 51 on the pass off the net
	•tip if trapped (along net or center court)

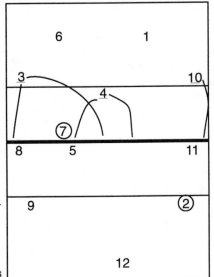

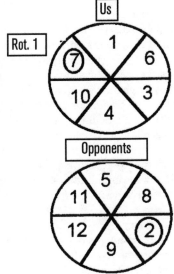

court before the middle blocker has a chance to close the block. It requires the setter to direct the middle hitter one way and then set the ball the opposite way. Since the opponent's middle blocker is big, the setter should only set the middle when the pass is off the net or when the middle blocker is out of position.

Matching Up With The Opponents

Normally, coaches think of match-ups as being front-row match-ups (e.g., the opposite vs. the outside hitter). Because of the way individual players rotate on the court, the best a coach can do when attempting to match up with the opponents is to have it work as they wish in two out of the three rotations. Experts will disagree about how a coach should select a match-up rotation with an opponent. Some think it is best to put your strengths against the opponent's strengths. For example, match up your best outside blocker (probably your opposite) with the opponent's best outside hitter. Others believe it is important to try to achieve a mis-match where you have a strong hitter on a weak blocker. The problem for most coaches is that the opponent's best hitter can also be their best blocker. If the opponent's best hitter is an outside hitter, you have a problem—one outside hitter usually cannot block an opposing outside hitter because of their respective positions on the court. This is when the challenge comes! Many times a coach will have to use the "trial and error" method.

Following are some basic suggestions for matching up with the opponents:

• If you have not seen the other team play, start in your strongest rotation. You can always change after the first game.

• If you win the game, stay the same (notice it rhymes!)

• If you lose the game, strongly consider "spinning the wheel" to get different match-ups—especially if your star hitter is getting blocked consistently.

• If you lose the game because of poor passing or serving–try some subs to strengthen those areas. You may not want to change the match-ups in this situation.

• If you lose the game because of poor match-ups, but do not want to change your rotations, try individual subs to strengthen the problem areas.

• If you have scouted the team and are deciding the match-ups prior to the start of the match, consider putting your best middle blocker opposite the opponent's best hitter. Also, put your best right-side blocker opposite their best outside hitter.

Scouting in Person vs. Scouting from Videotape

A good videotape of an opponent is the best friend a coach can have. A tape will give you endless opportunities to view the opponents as opposed to a one-shot view at courtside. Recently, the NCAA instituted a tape exchange policy for all women's teams qualifying for the Division I national championship. Specific guide-

lines are now in place for positioning of the camera (wide angle lens to see the entire court from behind the endline); quality of the tape (numbers on jerseys must be visible); and how the tape should be shipped.

Some computer programs are now available to use for scouting purposes. (These will be discussed at length in Chapter 8.) The program allows a coach to mark the rotations and put together a "rotational tape" so you have all of the play from the entire match viewed by rotation. For example, the program cuts and pastes all of the segments where the team is in rotation No. 5. It is an excellent tool for team viewing.

Scouting Your Own Team

Many of the best coaches use the scouting techniques presented in this chapter to scout their own team, in addition to their opponents. These technicians believe that a coach needs to know more about the team he is coaching than about the opponents. Scouting the opponents and knowing what it takes to win means little if the team cannot implement the plan. Russ Rose, the head women's volleyball coach at Penn State University, has the following philosophy about scouting. He spends the first one-third of the season scouting his own team so that he knows its strengths and weaknesses. During this period, practice time is spent improving his team's weaknesses. The second third of the season is spent developing the ability to attack other teams' weaknesses in general (e.g., a small blocker or a poor passer). Finally, during the last third of the season, practice time is spent on developing the ability to be successful against specific match-ups. For example, Rose might design a specific blocking and defensive scheme for an opposing middle hitter with definite attack tendencies. Regardless of a coach's individual philosophy for scouting opponents, it is critical that the coach be aware of the abilities of his own team and address those competitive needs first.

team to take advantage of its own strengths and minimize the strengths of the opponent. Do not plan to execute any tactics which your team cannot perform technically.

Summary

• Charting is one of the most effective ways to record the hitting tendencies, offense, defense and other subtleties of a specific team.

• Charting can be used by coaches, fans and media to enhance their knowledge and understanding of volleyball.

• Whenever possible, find a spot behind the court (on the endline) to view a match. This vantage point allows the viewer to have the best angle from which to watch the action on the court—especially the action at the net.

• For purposes of describing the location of a set along the net, the net is divided into nine equal sections, from antenna to antenna. These are numbered 1 through 9 going from left to right. The height of the set is described by a numbering system which tells the hitter how high above the net the set will travel.

• Serve reception offense and side-out offense are interchangeable terms used for describing a team's first play of the ball directly off serve reception.

• Transition offense is the term used to describe all of the attacking action after the initial pass, set and attack off serve reception.

• Floor defense is the term routinely used to describe the positioning of the non-blocking members of the defensive team on the court. Four types were discussed: perimeter, person-up, rotation and person across.

• The blocking system used by an opponent is important to know when planning a team's attack strategy. Study the blockers to find their strengths and weaknesses.

• The offensive plays used by the opponents are keys to devising a good defensive gameplan for a coming match.

• A good gameplan should allow your

Chapter 6

"Never tell people how to do things. Tell them what to do and they will surprise you with their ingenuity."
George Patton, U.S. general

Practice Planning

Developing a volleyball program takes a good, multi-faceted blueprint. One part of the coach's role is to serve the team effectively as a psychologist, a motivator, a teacher, a counselor, a tactician and an administrator. Another part of the coaching role is to organize the physical development of the players and the team. Planning practice sessions is where this organizational process starts. Knowing both the strengths and weaknesses of the team is important in planning practice sessions and statistics can be a valuable tool in this process of performance evaluation. Becoming a good coach depends on the ability to maximize strengths strategically and patiently improve and cope with weaknesses. Coaches can have access to hundreds of different statistics, yet, if they do not understand how to use them, the numbers are pointless.

One purpose of this chapter is to give some suggestions about putting the statistics that have been discussed to use. In addition to knowing the strengths and limitations of your team, it is important to know what level of performance is necessary to be successful. Study the statistics of the best teams in your conference or area and compare them with those of your team to determine which skill areas must be improved to increase success. This is where the team's physical development blueprint begins to take shape.

The situations discussed in this chapter deal with specific issues surrounding practice planning. Another purpose of this chapter is to provide charts for basic organization in long-range and daily practice planning.

Assessing Your Team

•Situation 1: You are the coach of a college team, Grandview, which has just completed a rather mediocre season. During the off-season you sit down with your staff to plan the off-season practice schedule. It is important to your job security and mental health that the staff plan a practice schedule to improve team performance.

▲Stage One - The first stage of this process will compare the team's performance with conference opponents in several skill areas. Suggested steps in the process include:

1. Gather all of the conference and team statistics for comparison.

2. Rank each team's performance within each skill area. Compare how your team ranked within each skill area.

3. Note the performance level of the conference champion, second- and third-place teams in all statistical areas. Determine which statistical areas have most influenced team success (e.g., hitting and blocking are two of the skills which most directly affect team success.)

4. Look at the difference between your team's rank in each area with the conference leaders. This should give you an idea about what statistical values your team needs to achieve in order to move up in the standings.

Table 1 presents the conference season statistics and shows where Grandview finished in relation to the rest of the conference in several statistical areas.

Following the steps outlined above, Grandview's coaching staff makes these observations about the conference statistics:

•The team must improve in several areas to reach the goal of finishing among the top three in the conference standings.

•With the exception of service aces, the team is in the "middle of the pack" in every category—approximately the same as the overall finish.

•Plainview won the conference championship and was ranked No. 2 in hitting efficiency, No. 1 in blocking and digs. Eastern finished No. 2 in the conference and ranked No. 1 in hitting efficiency, kills and assists and No. 2 in aces.

•Specific objectives and priorities

Table 1: Conference Season Statistics

Conference Season Statistics

Conference Finish	Hitting Eff.	%	Kills (per game)	Ave.	Blocks (per game)	Ave.
1. Plainview	1. Eastern	.287	1. Eastern	17.43	1. Plainview	3.02
2. Eastern	2. Plainview	.269	2. Valley St.	16.02	2. Midland	2.75
3. Midland	3. Valley St.	.265	3. Midland	15.44	3. Wesley	2.56
Valley State	4. Midland	.233	4. Plainview	15.40	4. Valley St.	2.55
5. Wesley	5. Grandview	.230	5. Grandview	14.98	5. Grandview	2.54
6. Grandview	6. Wesley	.205	6. Wesley	14.77	6. Heartland	2.53
7. Hillsborough	7. Hillsborough	.190	7. Southland	13.90	7. Southland	2.51
Mesa	8. Southland	.187	8. Hillsborough	13.78	8. Eastern	2.27
9. Southland	9. Lakeview	.181	9. Heartland	13.39	9. Lakeview	13.26
10. Lakeview	10. Heartland	.173	10. Lakeview	13.26	10. Hillsborough	1.95
11. Heartland	11. Mesa	.160	11. Mesa	12.98	11. Mesa	1.72

Aces (per game)	Ave.	Assists (per game)	Ave.	Digs (per game)	Ave.
1. Grandview	2.11	1. Eastern	15.28	1. Plainview	19.10
2. Eastern	1.99	2. Valley St.	13.88	2. Wesley	16.61
3. Lakeview	1.98	3. Plainview	13.82	3. Southland	15.87
4. Midland	1.88	4. Midland	13.33	4. Heartland	15.75
5. Wesley	1.84	5. Wesley	13.32	5. Midland	15.29
6. Soutland	1.82	6. Grandview	13.00	6. Eastern	15.14
7. Mesa	1.80	7. Hillsborough	11.85	7. Grandview	14.13
8. Valley St.	1.71	8. Heartland	11.67	8. Hillsborough	15.13
9. Plainview	1.61	9. Southland	11.59	9. Valley St.	15.03
10. Hillsborough	1.49	10. Lakeview	11.53	10. Mesa	14.68
11. Heartland	1.28	11. Mesa	11.23	11. Lakeview	14.58

will have to be addressed in practice to move the team in a positive direction toward enhanced performance.

▲Stage Two - The second stage in the process of designing a blueprint for team success is determining a set of priorities for improvement. Setting priorities is essential, since most coaches feel there is never enough time to accomplish everything. Based on an evaluation of the conference statistics, Grandview's coaching staff determines that hitting efficiency, blocking and team defense are the areas which require the most immediate attention. Since a majority of the team will be returning the following year, the coaching staff sets three priorities (goals) for concentration during off-season practice:

1) improve hitting efficiency by 30 points;
2) improve blocking by .5 blocks per game; and
3) improve team defense and increase to 17.13 digs per game.

The coach is happy with the serving (aces per game) and would like to maintain that ranking. Assists and kills should improve with the hitting efficiency. Accomplishing the three priorities should move Grandview up significantly in the conference standings.

▲Stage Three - The third stage of putting the overall plan for improvement into action is to decide how much time should be spent on each phase of the game. A suggestion is to formulate a pie chart depicting practice time based on the priorities which have been set. Figure 6-1 shows a pie chart representing the percentage of practice time which will be allotted to each phase of the game, based

Figure 6-1: Structuring Practice Time

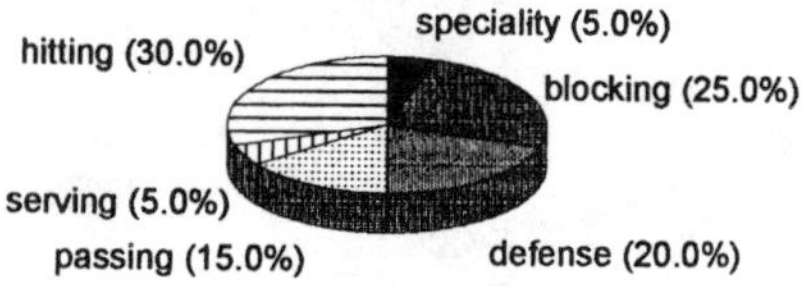

hitting (30.0%)
speciality (5.0%)
blocking (25.0%)
serving (5.0%)
passing (15.0%)
defense (20.0%)

on the priorities the coach has set. Grandview has a two-and-a-half-hour practice or 150 minutes. Taking out a half-hour for warm-up, cool down and stretching, the coach is left with 120 minutes of actual practice time. If the coach calculated the time to be spent on each phase based on the priorities, it could look something like this: 36 minutes for hitting; 30 minutes for blocking, 24 minutes for defense; 18 minutes for passing; and six minutes each for serving and spe-

cialty work. Of course, the coach could combine one or more of these areas into a certain time block. For example, the setter could be doing specialty work as part of the hitting emphasis. Serving could be included in the passing emphasis and so on. This is one example of how a coach could systematically structure practice time to accomplish the team goals.

A plan for dividing practice time by skill areas would be especially effective in the off-season, where the coach is more concerned with individual skills, not competition. During the competitive season, it is important to have more team-oriented drills, but the focus of these team drills could be on the player's individual skills as they relate to the overall team performance.

▲Stage Four - The fourth stage of the plan for improvement is to identify specific keys within each skill area which are needed for optimum individual performance. The Grandview coach must determine what specific aspects of each skill area need the most work (e.g., attacking during transition offense; attacking against a big block; footwork for the spiking approach; mechanics of hitting; etc.). In other words, specifically what does his team need to work on during its 36 minutes of hitting in each practice? To assist him in making this determination, the Grandview coach makes a chart to serve as a checklist. Figure 6-2 shows a list of proficiencies the Grandview coach wants to use in preparing to plan practices. Remember, his goals are to improve hitting efficiency, improve blocking and to improve overall team defense. Once the coach makes some determination about the cause(s) of the low hitting efficiency,

for example, a plan for addressing the problem(s) in practice directly can be made.

The Grandview coach needs to make some determination about whether the lack of proficiencies in the three areas above are related to a lack of individual skill by specific key players or a more general absence of knowledge about the needed skills. He will have to dedicate enough practice time to begin turning these deficiencies into proficiencies.

The Grandview coach determined that hitting efficiency is the single most important area for improvement. The domain of hitting efficiency can be further divided into areas such as transition offense (side-out offense) and serve reception offense. Going even further, the hitting efficiency, an area for improvement, can be subdivided to specific situations (e.g., hitting against a double block) and individual player performances in these specific situations. The Grandview coach can set up specific situations in practice and measure the player and team performance in these areas. Rotation by rotation, the deficiencies can be attacked and mastered. Drills which require measured success should be used.

▲Stage Five - Finally, it must be noted that many of the problem aspects of team performance can be related to other variables. Use the available team and individual statistics to identify the performance variables affecting each skill. For example, the area of hitting efficiency can be affected by performance in other skills. Some examples are:

•Passing efficiency: Affects the setter's ability to run the offense efficiently. Check for low team and individual pass-

Figure 6-2: Checklist for Individual Player Proficiency

	Physical Skills	Mental/Situational Skills
Hitting Efficiency	-spiking approach	-reading the defense
	-spiking mechanics	-reading the block
	-shot selection	-specific game situations based on score, point vs. side-out, etc.
	-transition	-offensive strategy
Blocking	-blocking mechanics	-reading the setter
	-setting/closing block	-reading the hitter
	-transition	-specific game strategies
	-tactics on play-sets	
Team Defense	-base position	-reading the setter
	-transition/positioning	-reading the hitter
	-digging mechanics	-position around block
	-emergency skills	-specific game strategies
	-hitter coverage	

ing efficiencies.

•Setting proficiency - Affects the hitter's effectiveness; the offense may be too complicated for the skill level of the setter; or the offense may not be diverse enough for the hitter's abilities. Check the combined performance of the setter(s) and the hitters using the Set Selection Chart.

•Rotation problems: The alignment of the players on the court may not be as advantageous as it could be to balance the attack or the team may suffer because of one or two weak rotations. Check for rotations with low points per rotation statistics.

The situation presented here shows one way of addressing team statistical issues by specifically defining team and individual proficiencies which are needed. Improving team performance requires a thorough review of the statistics for each player, then setting objective, measurable proficiencies for each skill area. The same would be done for the team as a whole. Each practice needs to set out definite objectives which move the team toward the overall goals. Players seem to respond best when they understand this process. Give them reasons for each objective. It is not a simple process and takes a time commitment from the coach to lay the blueprint.

•Situation 2: To assess the strengths and weaknesses of his team further, the Grandview coach used a "Point Scoring Chart" (Appendix, Form 23) during the season. This chart is designed to give a point-by-point summary of scoring by both Grandview and the opponents in each game. Figure 6-3 (page 60) shows an example of a Point Scoring Chart for a game between Grandview and Plainview. A coach or manager can keep the chart on the bench. The key at the bottom gives abbreviations to use in noting how points were scored. On the bottom of the chart, a game summary shows points scored for the team by kills, aces, stuff blocks and opponent errors. The summary also shows the points scored against the team by kills, aces, stuff blocks and Grandview errors. At the end of the game, the statistician totals the number of points scored in each category of the summary.

Figure 6-3 shows that Plainview won the game, 15-8. Grandview's first point was scored because of an attack error out of the back row by No. 10 from Plainview. The second point scored by Grandview

came on a stuff block of Plainview's No. 10 by two Grandview players, Nos. 6 and 9. The third point for Grandview was scored on a kill by the outside hitter, No. 13. In this specific game, Grandview scored only four of its eight points (50 percent) on positive actions—four were scored as a result of opponent errors. Plainview, on the other hand, scored 11 of its 15 points (73 percent) because of positive actions. The most obvious difference in point scoring came in the area of kills. Plainview scored eight points on its own kills, while Grandview scored only one point. If this trend were present throughout the season, the Grandview coach has one more fact to reinforce his theory that hitting efficiency should be the No. 1 priority for team improvement.

Drills for Practice

Many beginning coaches do not realize that the best drills they can use are those made up specifically for their own team. Drill concepts can be borrowed from other coaches, but rarely will one coach's drill be designed to meet the specific needs of another person's team. Drills that will improve the performance of the team in game situations should be done—and not merely to take up practice time. To design a team or individual drill, it is necessary to:

•Define the specific problem area (e.g., during a long rally, the players get out of position and end up being disorganized).

•Set up a practice situation which is similar to the game situation where the problem occurs (e.g., continuously sending balls over the net from a controlled attack or coach's tosses and making the team successfully convert to offense).

•Outline the problem for the team, giving the players a solution or way to solve it—some coaches prefer to have the individual or team offer a solution (e.g., immediately get back to base positions each time the ball goes across the net).

•Set expectations or goals for the team (e.g., the team must convert by getting three good attacks in a row before rotating positions).

•Evaluate the team performance and get player feedback.

Well-planned practices lead to success on the court. Therefore, all types of drills used in practice should, as much as possible, resemble game-like situations the players will face during competition.

Restrict slower paced, teaching drills to small amounts of practice time. The drills a coach uses will dictate the tempo of practice and the game of volleyball is normally very fast-paced. Players find it very difficult to go from a slow-paced practice to actual competition with a much faster tempo.

Types of Drills

1. Teaching drills: Skill progressions, movement patterns, emphasis on mechanics, slower paced (e.g., teaching the spike).

2. Rapid-fire drills: The goal is to have as many contacts as possible, little emphasis on teaching, fast tempo (e.g., coach on one player—rapid digging).

3. Crisis drills: Emphasis on performing skills under stress, very fast tempo (e.g., team defense with constant attacks from the opposing side of the net).

4. Flow of play drills: Combines two or more skills with a game-like tempo (e.g., team serve reception and play out with a pass, set and attack).

Drill Organization

1. Coach-centered drills: The coach is tossing balls and/or controlling the pace of the drill; the coach initiates the drill and keeps it going. Figure 6-4 shows a coach-centered drill, where the coach starts and conducts the entire drill. The object of the drill is to pass a ball to the target area while running forward.

2. Player-centered drills: The players initiate the drill and keep it going;

Figure 6-4: Run Throughs to Target

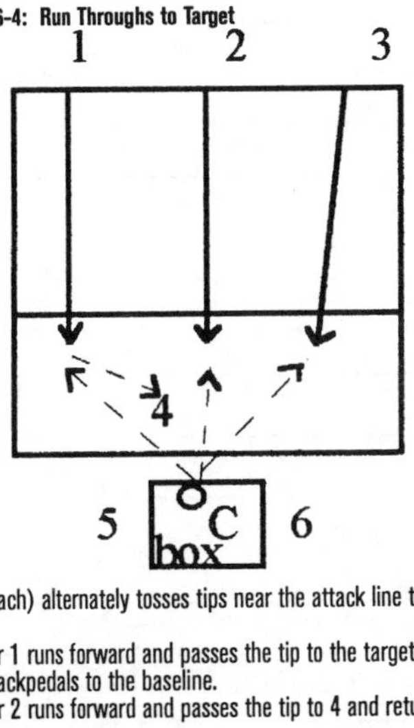

•C (coach) alternately tosses tips near the attack line to 1, 2 and 3.
•Player 1 runs forward and passes the tip to the target (4), then backpedals to the baseline.
•Player 2 runs forward and passes the tip to 4 and returns to baseline.
•Player 3 runs forward to pass the tip to 4 and returns to baseline.
•Players 4, 5 and 6 shag and hand balls to the coach.
•The drill is fast-paced with the goal of a certain number of good passes to target.

POINT SCORING CHART

Grandview   VS.   Plainview   Game #   3   Date: October 27

Team: Grandview   **Team:**   Plainview

Type of Play	Player #	Point Number	Type of Play	Player #
AE backrow	10	1	K on right cross	5
SB on #10	6 & 9	2	A on #12	3
K on outside	13	3	AE	13
SB on #4	8	4	SB on #12	10
A on #5	6	5	K on outside	4
BHE	3	6	K in middle	2
AE	5	7	AE	9
NV	7	8	K on right cross	5
		9	AE	6
		10	K on outside	11
		11	SB on #13	2 & 3
		12	K in middle	2
		13	K on outside	4
		14	BHE	7
		15	K on dump	3
		16		
		17		
		18		
		19		
		20		
		21		
		22		
		23		
		24		
		25		
		26		
		27		
		28		
		29		
		30		

GAME SUMMARY

Points For

Type	# Points
Kill	1
Ace	1
Stuff Block	2
Opponent Error	4

Points Against

Type	#Points
Kill	8
Ace	1
Stuff Block	2
Our Error	4

Key

K = Kill	SB = Stuff Block	BHE = Ball Handling Error	O = Overlap Error
A = Ace	NV = Net Violation	SE = Service Error	AE = Attack Error

Figure 6-5: Cross-court Hit and Dig for Ball Control

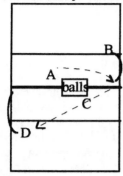

•A sets ball outside to B
•B approaches and hits cross-court to D (A and B switch places)
•D digs the ball to C
•C sets back to D
•D hits cross-court to A (C and D switch places)
•The goal of this drill is to keep the ball in play continuously back and forth across the net. If a mistake is made, players in the setting position enter a ball.

players control the tempo of the drill. Figure 6-5 shows a player-centered drill where the object of the drill is for the players to control hit the ball cross-court continuously.

3. Coach-initiated drills: The coach starts the drill with the first contact and play is allowed to follow to its natural conclusion. Figure 6-6 shows a coach-initiated drill where the coach enters the

Figure 6-6: Back-row Attack King of the Hill

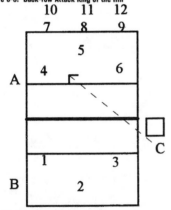

•Coach enters a free ball to Side A.
•Players on side A pass, set and back-row attack to side B.
•Players on side B dig, set and back-row attack to side A.
•Play continues until the ball is dead.
•The winners stay or move to side B; a new team moves into side B.
•The losers retrieve the ball and get in line behind side B.
•A point is scored by the team when they win while on side B.

first ball (free ball) and the play continues until the ball is dead. The coach then enters another ball for the next group and can control the tempo by the speed at which the ball is entered.

4. Player-centered/coach-initiated drills: The players start the drill with a serve and the coach initiates a second sequence by entering a free ball. Players control the tempo while the ball is in play.

The coach controls the overall pace of the drill by the speed at which the free balls are entered. Figure 6-7 shows a player-centered/coach-initiated drill focusing on team defense for the players on one side of the net ("second team") and team of-

Figure 6-7: Wash Drill

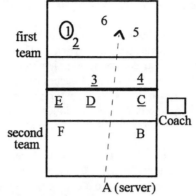

•Player A serves to the first team.
•The first team passes, sets and attacks.
•The second team defends and plays out.
•The second team scores; they receive a big point and serve again.
•If the first team scores off serve reception, they get a little point and receive a free ball from the coach; if they score again they receive a big point. If the second team wins the free ball it is a wash and the second team serves again.
•Every time a team receives a big point, they rotate one position.
•The first team to score six big points wins.
•The coach may wish to penalize the second team for missed serves.
•The coach could play the entire game in one rotation if it is a problem rotation.

fense for the players on the other side of the net ("first team"). This particular drill uses the "wash" scoring system and gives an advantage to the "second team."

Duration of Drills

1. Timed: The drill runs for a set amount of time.

2. Successful repetitions: The team or individual must complete a set number of successful repetitions to complete the drill.

3. Time/repetitions: The team or player must complete a successful number of repetitions in a specific amount of time.

4. Consecutive successful repetitions: The team or individual must complete a set number of successful repetitions in a row; the count starts over each time an error or an unsuccessful play is made.

Scoring for Team Drills

1. Fast Score or Rally Score: A point is scored by the team winning the rally each time the ball is served.

2. Handicaps: One team starts with a greater number of points (e.g., the first team starts the drill with nine points and the second team starts with 12 points—the first team to 15 wins).

3. Consecutive points burden: A team must score two or more points in a row to get credit for one point (e.g., the first team must score twice in a row to get one point and the second team has normal scoring).

4. Wash drills: Big points and little points (e.g., the receiving team must convert a serve reception for a "little point" and a free ball for a second little point in order to score a "big point").

Phases of Practice

Most practices follow a normal pattern beginning with warm-up and ending with a cool-down. Between the warm-up and cool down, coaches can choose to spend varying amounts of time on teaching, repetitive foundation work, team-oriented work and game situation work. Coaches should consider the following segments as important aspects of a practice session:

•Warm-up - Players need to perform enough volleyball-related activity to raise the core body temperature one degree (break a sweat) before stretching.

•Foundation work - Basic individual skills training.

•Multiple skill work - Training which combines several skills in game-related situations—this can be accomplished in small groups or by grouping players who play similar positions together (e.g., middle hitters and setters work together on quick attacks; outside hitters work together on back-court defense).

•Teamwork - Focus is one the entire team working together in game situations—the coach should control the focus, not merely have an intra-squad scrimmage.

•Pressure or stress work - Individual players or the entire team must successfully perform techniques or tactics in pressure situations.

•Cool-down - Players should be allowed to take a few minutes to slow down their heart rate and do some gentle stretching.

The amount of time spent on individual and team skills largely depends on the time of year the practice takes place. The amount of conditioning which takes place in a practice session also depends on the time of year and the amount of time outside practice a coach has to conduct individual conditioning. It may be necessary to include some conditioning in practice. However, a well-run practice with a fast tempo can serve as a two-hour conditioning session by itself! Experts generally agree that preseason and early season should devote larger amounts of practice time to individual skills work and foundation work. As the middle of the season approaches, however, the emphasis should shift to more team-oriented work and situational drills. Late in the season and during post-season tournament competition, the emphasis shifts almost exclusively to team-oriented training. At this point, foundation work and individual skill training should not take much practice time.

Practice Planning Forms
Weekly Practice Planner - Appendix, Form 24

Planning practices is one of the most important tasks for the coach. Coaches should make a general plan (season overview) before the season starts; often, however, this plan will have to be modified as the season progresses. Until the first competition, it is difficult to know how the team will compete and what areas of team and individual play will need the most work. Therefore, the weekly plan becomes more critical to the ultimate success of the team. Statistics taken during competition become important in helping the coach to identify areas where improvement is needed. These statistics should help shape the plans for the coming week. The statistics of the upcoming opponents should also assist the coach in formulating a gameplan for the match. Figure 6-8 shows an example of a weekly plan for the middle of the competitive season.

Daily Practice Plan - Appendix, Form 25

The Daily Practice Plan form gives the coach a standardized form to use for individual practices. It should be used in conjunction with the Weekly Practice Plan. If the weekly form is completed at the beginning of each week, the coach has a better chance of making sure to cover all of the skill work necessary to be ready for upcoming competition. Some coaches like to post practice plans ahead of time so players are informed about what to expect in practice. Such a policy can be helpful to players who set daily goals for practice.

Figure 6-9 (page 64) shows a two-hour practice. Note that the practice is planned using the goals laid out for Tuesday, Oct. 10, as shown in Figure 6-8. Remember, the coach has used notes and statistics from previous competitions to put together the weekly plan.

Team Bulletin - Appendix, Form 26

This is a simple form that can be used to facilitate communication between the coach and the team. Coaches can post notices in the locker room for important dates, meeting times, reminders or a variety of items.

Volleyball Calendar - Appendix, Form 27

The volleyball calendar is a handy form for the coach to use as a planner for scheduling. It can also be used to compile a listing of important times, dates and events, then be distributed to team members. Players can use this tool in planning for academic events, such as tests and papers, as well as for their athletic schedule. Time management is an important concept for players to learn at an early age.

Player Conference Outline - Appendix, Form 29

One of the most common complaints players often express about a coach is the coach's lack of understanding about the player's concerns. The player conference outline is presented as a suggested tool for facilitating one-on-one meetings between the player and the coach. The form is presented to the players several days before the scheduled conference. Players are asked to complete the form before attending the conference. Several important topics are presented on the form in an attempt to encourage the player to take an active role in discussion during the conference. Coaches can increase communication between themselves and the players when they give players a chance to participate in constructive evaluation of a player's role on the team and personal goals. While honest discussion is often difficult, it almost always will enhance and nurture the player's growth. Coaches should try to be open to constructive criticism from individual players about team concerns and issues. Sports psychologists suggest that coaches meet individually with players as often as reasonably possible during the season and at the conclusion of the season.

Conclusion

• Statistics can be used to assess the competitive strength of a team. Ranking common opponents in different statistical categories and comparing those rankings with overall success will shed some light on which statistical areas appear to be most important to competitive team success. This process can assist coaches in developing specific statistical priorities for improving team competitiveness.

• Coaches should structure practice time to allow for improvement in statistical areas which have been identified as important to overall competitive strength.

• Coaches should develop a checklist of physical and mental proficiencies which are needed to improve individual performance. This process will allow coaches to plan practices which develop competencies in specific skill areas.

• Systematic weekly and daily practice planning will help ensure that the overall competitive success of the team is maximized.

WEEKLY PRACTICE PLANNER

Date   *October 9 - 14 (mid season)*

Day	Primary Focus Team	Primary Focus Individual	Seconday Focus Team	Seconday Focus Individual

Monday	Defense:
	  Attack from OH
	  Attack from MH
	  Attack from RS
	  Backrow attack
		Defense:
		  Reading hitters
		  Moving to position
		  Control dig
			Down block &
			  freeball transition
			  (offense)
				Emergency ball
				control skills

Tuesday	Transition:
	  Defense to offense
	  Rotations 1, 4 & 5
		Ball Control:
		  Digging
		  Attack (cross court)
			Serve Reception:
			  Rotations 1, 4, &5
				Serving to area
				Passing to target

Wednesday	Blocking assignments
	vs. assorted
	combination plays
		Blocking:
		  Setting the block
		  Closing the block
		  Communication
		  Pennetration
			Backrow adjustments
			for
			combination plays
				Digging around
				the block

Thursday	Focus on strengths and weaknesses of upcoming opponent--
	
	Serve Reception:
	  Alternate formations
	  Serve reception off.
	  (All rotations)
		Serving to areas
		Passing topsin &
		float serves
			Transition:
			  Serve rec. to defense
			  Blocking to offense
				Attacking:
				  Hitting around block
				  Hitting shots

Friday	Travel and video tape review ---			

Saturday	Matches ----------------
	
	Goal: improve transition
	  offense--hold
	  opponents to
	  .6 pts per rotation
			Goal: improve serve
			  receive offense--
			  .9 pts per rotation
			  in rot. 1, 4 & 5	

Day	Notes and Special Announcements

DAILY PRACTICE PLAN

Date <u>Oct. 10</u>   (Midseason)   ***Primary Focus***   <u>Transition from defense to offense</u>

<u>Time</u>   <u>*Warm-Up*</u>

5	a. footwork - def. position to spike approach
5	b. ball handling - partner digging from transition
5	c. blocking - hands and arm work
5	d. backrow attack - King of the Hill
10	e. stretching

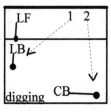
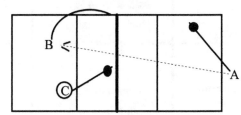

<u>*Individual Skills*</u>

15   Serve, pass, set and hit:

A serves to B (A moves to assigned def. pos.)
B passes to C (C plays setter & penetrates)
C sets to B
B hits to area where A is playing
A digs, then goes back to serve again
Goal: 3 good passes & hits in a row then
         rotate.

Players serve & move to assigned def.
positions and passers pass from normal
passing positions then hit from normal attack
areas (i.e. right, left, middle)

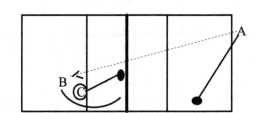

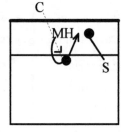

<u>*Positional/Group Work*</u>

15   a. freeball transition hitting w/ setters
       C toss freeball (hitter in def. position)
       hitter transitions, passes, approach, hit
       setter transitions from RB
       Goal: 3 good hits in a row

15   b. defensive transition hitting (side-out off)
       C toss to S1
       S1 sets to OH or RS
       Hitters must hit cross court (to RS or OH)
       Deffense digs and S2 sets OH, RS, MH
       Goal: 2 good transitions in a row

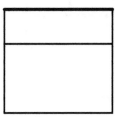
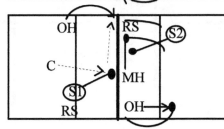

<u>*Team Drills/Competition*</u>

30   Wash: Defense to Offense
       B = 2nd team   A = 1st team
       Team B serves to team A
       Team A plays it out
       If A scores they get freeball (C)
       Goal: 6 pt. games w/ A winning
       big pt. = sr + freeball for A's
       big pt. = score on serve for B's

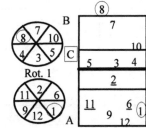
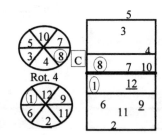

10   <u>*Cool Down*</u>:   slow jog around gym and stretch

5   <u>*Announcements*</u>:   leave for games at 11:00 am on Friday;   bring both uniform shirts

Chapter 7

"Hit 'em where they ain't."
"Wee" Willie Keeler, American baseball player

Creating a Charting Scheme

Contributed by Ravi Narasimhan

The preceding chapters have introduced a number of methods that are useful in recording and analyzing performances on the volleyball court. The examples and chart fragments are all based on a definition of sets and a few simple graphical elements which represent plays and outcomes. There are many charting schemes in use, each well-suited to examining a particular aspect of the game. The sheer volume of data in a completed chart can be intimidating at first glance. This, however, is misleading. The most beautiful structures are often built with a small set of tools, a simple plan and systematic execution. Good charts are a perfect example.

Designing a chart and developing a charting plan first require a goal. For example, finding where the opponents are and the offense they like to run can be vital to implementing Keeler's ungrammatical — yet sage — advice in the heat of battle. This chapter outlines, in steps, how to build charts that show the offensive tendencies and scoring patterns of one team in a match. The ideas and notational conventions from the previous chapters will form the toolbox for this project. Within each charting scheme, concentrate on finding the hitters and diagramming the attack. The task will begin with a simple, side-out only chart with few annotations and develop to include passing rankings, sets and plays, points scored and allowed, as well as other notes.

The chapter concludes with an actual charting scheme used by many top-level collegiate teams in the United States. Specific examples include those from the 1996 Olympic men's gold medal match between Holland and Italy — a match considered by many to be the finest ever played.

The Fan's Chart

Good charting requires noticing as much ball and player movement as possible and dispassionately writing down the results. As noted earlier, an endline seat is very good for this purpose. Watching and recording one team's actions in serve receive is a good way to get practice with the various steps involved. Figure 7-1 shows a sample chart blank with six courts arranged in two rows of three columns. Plays can be diagrammed in the court, one for each of the team's six rotations.

Finding the Hitters

The first step is to find the front-row hitters and can be done when the team being charted is serving. Simply jot down the numbers of the three players at the net. When the team goes back to receive

Figure 7-1: A Bare-bones Chart Blank

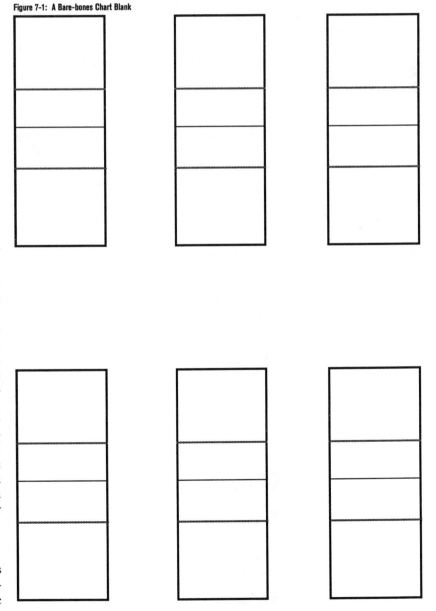

serve, note the locations of the front-row players on the chart. One commonly used scheme is to underline the front-row hitters and circle the setter.

Until very recently, men's teams have used two outside hitters, sometimes called swing hitters, to pass a majority of serves. The advent of the jump serve has led to adding a third passer in most rotations. Women's teams typically use a three-person receive alignment whereby different sets of three players pass in different rotations.

Most teams also run the 5-1 offense with one setter and five hitters. This means that there will be three rotations where there are only two hitters in the front row. Therefore, it is important to know the location of the player opposite the setter, since he/she will likely get a lot of sets in the back row. The left side of Figure 7-2 shows the rotation wheel for the two-passer offense, with SW referring to swing hitters; M the middles; and Opp the "big gun." The best swing hitter and middle are shown as SW1 and M1, respectively. The right side of Figure 7-2 shows an evolutionary step in men's volleyball, whereby defenses have begun to adjust to the opposite, who can terminate from the front or back row. Here, the best passer (P) is moved opposite the setter and is expected to shoulder — albeit with some help — a very heavy load receiving

serve. This allows two big hitters to be put into the O1 and O2 positions, where O refers now to a generic outside hitter.

Figure 7-3 shows one way to denote, for example, Holland's six serve-receive rotations. The choice of where to begin recording and the direction of rotation is up to the chart-taker. It is certainly possible to write down all six players in each rotation. This trades off completeness against legibility and is also up to the chart-taker.

Diagramming the Serve Receive Attack

There is a frenzy of activity on both sides after the ball has been served. The serving team's blockers will usually switch positions and the back-row players will accommodate the server moving to his/her defensive spot. This is even moreso the case for the receiving team. The setter breaks to his/her position along the net; one passer moves to the ball; the balance get to their hitting and coverage positions. The ball is set and someone takes a swing at it. The chart-taker notes and diagrams the approach, set, hitter, point of attack and result, kill, error, blocked ball or dug ball. Figure 5-1 introduced a way of referring to sets, Figure 5-9 a way to draw the play.

The Approach

For the outside and back-row hitters, coaches are mostly interested in the direction of the hit and the result. The middle attacker presents some additional elements such as the middle hitter's approach path; whether the hitter contacts the ball in front of or behind the setter; and whether the ball is hit along the direction of approach ("swinging away") or against the direction of approach ("cutback"). The speed of the quick attack makes this information necessary so that the blockers may be positioned accordingly. If the passing is good and the middle can hit along either direction, then the defense is in for a long match.

The chart-taker must therefore keep the middle hitter in focus and note in his/her mind which way the middle comes in. Quicksets behind the setter may be noted with a small "b" near the point of attack. In women's volleyball, the backslide (backset with a one-foot takeoff by the hitter) is a common play and is run at various positions along the net. A beginner may initially treat the middle as any other hitter, focusing first on point of attack and result. Adding the approach can be done after accumulating some experience. Figure 7-4 shows some of the paths taken by Dutch middle hitters Bas van de Goor (No. 9) and Henk Jan Held (No. 3).

Figure 7-2: Possible Evolution of Roles

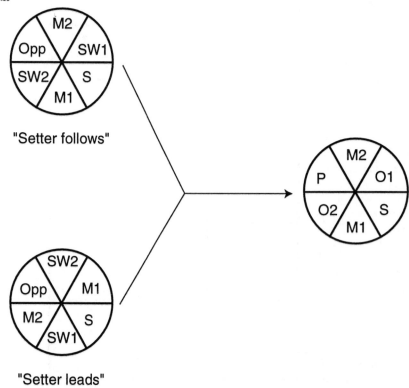

"Setter follows"

"Setter leads"

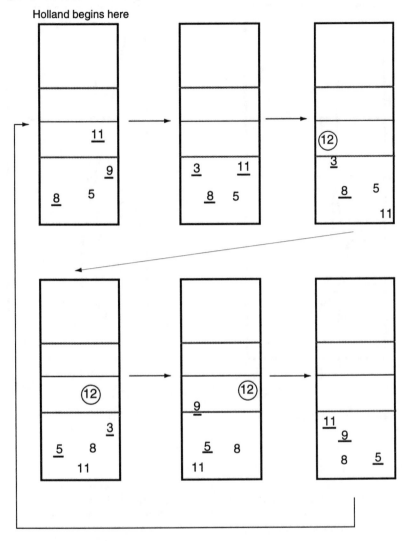

Figure 7-3: Holland's Six Serve Receive Alignments

Holland begins here

the setter choosing the one with the better chance of beating the block.

A popular instance is the front-row "x" play. The name "x" arises from the crossing paths of the middle hitter and one of the outside hitters in the front row. The setter has to decide whether the blockers are committing to the first player in. If so, the second hitter gets the ball. If the blockers stay down or "read" the first hitter, the quickset has a better chance of succeeding. Diagram this play as any other, marking a small "x" near the point of attack.

The combination play in transition is especially fun to watch, although few teams have the ball control to execute it effectively. With the advent of the 6'8" "big hitter" (or "thug" - see dictionary in appendix) in men's volleyball, the back-row combination is becoming popular. Indeed, an attack line at 3 meters is no impediment to a player of that size. The middle attacker goes in for the quick; the back-row attacker comes into the B/C region, known in the United States as a "pipe." Note that coaches will often disagree whether these back-row plays are indeed combinations which imply some specific timing between the two attackers. This is one of many judgment calls in charting. If a coach delegates this responsibility to someone else, both parties must agree in advance on what does and does not constitute a combination play. Figure 7-5 (page 70) shows some examples of front-row and front-row/back-row combinations.

A Practice Run

Figure 7-3 shows Holland's serve receive alignments. Table 1 (page 70) contains a roster and Table 2 (page 70) contains a list of plays specified by rotation as executed by Holland in game No. 3. Diagram these plays in and compare them with Figure 7-6 (page 71).

This chart is easy to teach and simple to take. It can be a good first step for someone new to volleyball, especially fans, toward seeing the game as more than a disjointed collection of attacks. Showing the steps to fans in a pre-match "chalk talk" and supplying some blank forms is one possible way to cultivate interest in the sport.

Shorthand Notation of Plays

A chart is a parallel, all-at-once representation of a match. While different colors can refer to different games, there

Figure 7-4: Dutch Middle Hitter Approaches

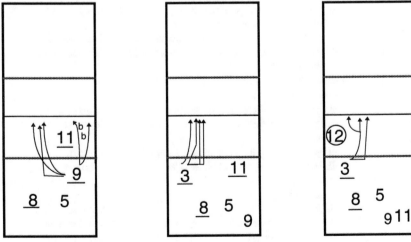

The Combination

Most modern volleyball offenses involve running many hitters "into the pattern." A powerful manifestation of this is the combination play in which two hitters come in, one behind the other, with

Figure 7-5: Front-Row and Back-row Combination Plays

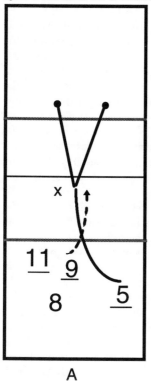

A

Front row X
No. 9 hits quick - first tempo
No. 5 hits second tempo

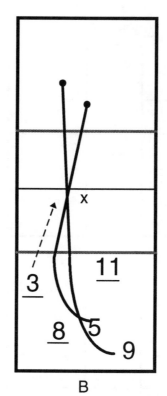

B

No. 3 hits quick

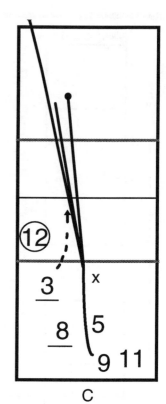

C

Back row/front row combo

No. 3 hits quick
No. 9 hits "pipe"

Table 1

Number	Name	Position
3	Henk Jan Held	Middle Blocker
5	Guido Gortzen	Outside Hitter
8	Ron Zwerver	Outside Hitter
9	Bas van de Goor	Middle Blocker
11	Olof van der Meulen	Opposite
12	Peter Blange	Setter

Table 2

Rotation	Play	Result of Rally
2	•Good pass, leftside to No. 8, hits seam, touched and dug	Italy scores
	•Marginal pass, fast backset to No. 11, offspeed shot into middle of the court, touched and dug	Holland sides out
3	•Good pass, quickset to No. 3, touched but falls	Holland sides out
4	•Poor pass, high ball to No. 8 on left side, hits hard cross-court and converts	Holland sides out
5	•Good pass, No. 3 runs at the setter, hops away, hits quickset against approach and converts	Holland sides out
6	•Marginal pass, shoot set to No. 9, hits a long approach and kills	Holland sides out
1	•Good pass, No. 9 comes quick, No. 5 comes behind on the combination. No. 5 is set and kills.	Holland sides out
2	•Good pass, first tempo set to No. 8 on left side, hits cross-court and is dug	Italy scores
	•Bad pass, high left side to No. 8, hits hard cross-court, dug	Holland sides out
3	•Bad pass, bumpset rightside to No. 11, hits hard cross-court, blocked	Italy scores
	•Marginal pass, pipe to No. 9, blocked back, dug by Holland	Italy scores
	•Marginal pass, second tempo set leftside to No. 8, hits cross-court, dug	Italy scores
	•Ace in area 5	Italy scores
	•Service error	Holland sides out
4	•Good pass, back-row to No. 11 in D zone, hits the seam	Holland sides out
5	•Good pass, shoot set to No. 3, hits with approach and terminates	Holland sides out
6	•Good pass, back-row to No. 11 in D zone, kills into area 5	Holland sides out
1	•Good pass, quickset to No. 9, touched and dug	Holland sides out

Figure 7-6: The First Few Side-out Rotations of Holland in Game No. 3

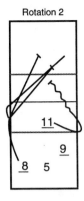

Rotation 2

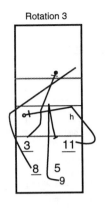

Rotation 3

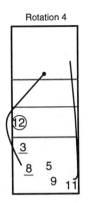

Rotation 4

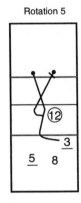

Rotation 5

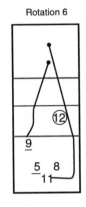

Rotation 6

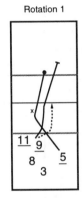

Rotation 1

passes, those not made by the setter or anything in which the hitter's natural rhythm is disrupted. These "high balls" can be noted with a small "h" in front of the set.

Ranking the Pass

The left two columns in the tabular form can be used to rank the pass and the passer, respectively. Every row of the table will therefore contain passing, as well as hitting information, which is very useful in identifying a setter's tendencies. Consider again Henk Jan Held's successful middle attack; this implies a good pass (a "3") by one of the receivers, e.g., Guideo Gortzen (No. 5). The form would then read:

3	5	51 3 +	

Keeping Score

A team can only lose points on serve receive. Identifying particularly bad rotations can be valuable for developing serving and defensive plans. This can be done in two places: in the fourth column of the tabular form and in the area below the chart as shown in Figure 7-7. If a play results in a side-out, note the pass ranking, passer and play and move to the next rotation as required. If a play results in a point being lost, the score can be recorded in the fourth column. A note can also be made in the area below the court. The redundancy makes sense if the chart-taker keeps a tally whenever the team sides out. This allows an easy computation of points per rotation.

Suppose that Holland were receiving serve while leading 12-9 when van der Meulen (No. 11) was blocked on the D ball, as was the case in the first game. The score then becomes 12-10. Given that the play was made on another good pass by Gortzen (No. 5), the completed row on the form would read:

3	5	D 11 b	12-10

Game to Game

At the end of every game, the teams change sides and often come out in different rotations, occasionally with different personnel. Identify the substitutes, if any, and begin recording in the correct rotation. If there is a pause between games, look over the "take." If there are any particularly bad rotations, one side or

is no way to tell the sequence of sets within a game and no way to tell in which sequence the lines were drawn. A complimentary "serial" data stream is needed. Fortunately, there is extra space in the chart blank for just such an emergency. Figure 7-7 shows an added tabular form, the third column of which can be used to record a set, the hitter and the result. Jotting this information after diagramming a play comes with very little practice. There is a surprisingly large amount of "dead time" in volleyball matches — plenty of time to take these and other notes.

A commonly used scheme for noting the result of an attack is:

- + = successful attack (ball put away, blockers in the net, etc.);
- 0 = dug ball, play continues;
- - = error (ball lands out of play area, hits the antenna, hitter is in the net, etc.);
- b = successful block by opponent (ball is blocked down and in the court).

For example, suppose middle hitter Henk Jan Held (No. 3) hit a 51 set

down for a kill. The form would read:

		51 3 +	

If opposite Olof van der Meulen (No. 11) hit a back-row ball from the D zone and got blocked, the notation would be:

		D 11 b	

Many coaches wish to know which sets are "emergencies" — those off of bad

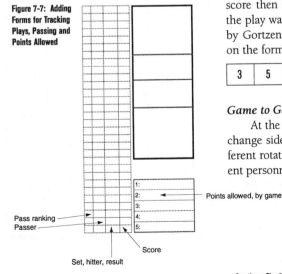

Figure 7-7: Adding Forms for Tracking Plays, Passing and Points Allowed

Points allowed, by game

Pass ranking
Passer

Score

Set, hitter, result

the other will try to adjust. Chart the first game in pencil so that errors may be erased. Chart subsequent games in a different color for each game.

The side change forces a mental inversion of player positions. The right-side hitter is now across the net on the left side and so forth. Of all of the varied aspects of charting, this probably requires the most practice. Remember to describe the ball's trajectory accurately on the chart, especially on the middle attack. It is usually possible to change sides, although many prefer to be as inconspicuous as possible when charting and scouting an opponent.

Transition

A side-out only chart can show what a team will do when it is allowed to run its offense. For many coaches, this will be sufficient information upon which to base decisions, either about an opponent being scouted or about their own teams. Adding information about transition is, however, valuable. It can identify particularly good point scoring rotations and provide information on what setters and hitters do in less-controlled situations.

An easy way to add space for transition plays is to reserve one half of the chart for this purpose. This requires two pages to accommodate all six rotations. Figure 7-8 shows a schematic implementation of this idea omitting, *for the moment*, tabular forms for plays and scoring. Each column represents one rotation: the top court is for transition, the bottom court is for serve-receive-attack. The top court is smaller since there are usually many more plays in serve receive than there are in transition. Some additional chart elements are shown. The spaces below the transition court may be used to record the positions of the blockers before and after the serve and the number of the server. Just above the serve receive court are five boxes. Each one may contain the number of the server from the opposing team. These may then be used to determine the rotation order of the opponent in each game. The figure also shows a detailed example of how to move from one part of the chart to another. Figure 7-9 shows how to go from page to page so that all six rotations may be represented.

The top court is used when:

• the team being charted is serving; and
• when the team being charted has completed its serve receive attack and is

Figure 7-8: Adding Transition and Zigzagging from Serve to Serve Receive

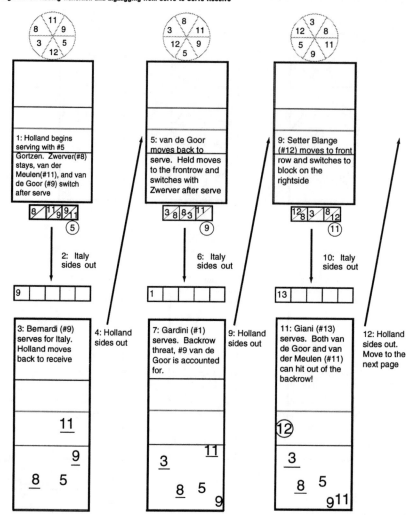

Figure 7-9: Using Two Sheets to Get Side-out and Transition Plays in All Six Rotations

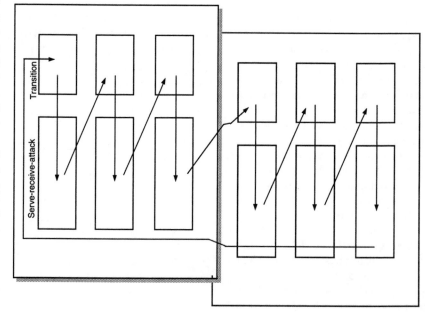

in the middle of a rally.

The bottom court is used when:

• the team being charted receives serve and mounts its first attack based on that reception.

The rally described below occurred in game No. 1 of the 1996 men's Olympic gold medal match and Figure 7-10 shows how to implement it based on the scheme described above: Dutch middle hitter van de Goor (No. 9) has moved into the passing rotation to help defend against

Figure 7-10: An Example of How to Go From Serve Receive to Transition

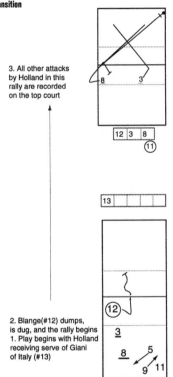

3. All other attacks by Holland in this rally are recorded on the top court

2. Blange(#12) dumps, is dug, and the rally begins
1. Play begins with Holland receiving serve of Giani of Italy (#13)

the jump serve of Italy's Andrea Giani (No. 13). Gortzen (No. 5) passes high and tight to the net; the setter Blange (No. 12) dumps the ball "on two" and is touched and dug by Italian defenders. van de Goor digs the high ball attack of Luca Cantagalli (No. 10); Blange sets Ron Zwerver (No. 8) on the left side and covers the attack, which is blocked back into the court. Zwerver is set again on the left side, this time by Held (No. 3) and his hard, cross-court shot is dug by Cantagalli and pushed over into the deep right corner by Lorenzo Bernardi (No. 9). van der Meulen (No. 11) digs to Blange, who sets Held in the middle and his cutback is dug in right back by Giani, off one arm and far outside the court. This ball is chased down and once again pushed over by Bernardi, this time to deep left back, where Gortzen takes it with his hands

back to Blange. Held and van de Goor run the front/back combination play; Blange sets a 12 to Zwerver, who hits "high hands" cross-court off a well-formed block and sides out.

The bottom court contains one play: the dump attempt by Blange. All of the other plays in the rally are recorded on the top court.

Due to blocking and defensive alignments, hitters may be in unusual areas in transition. If there is a prolonged rally, the chart-taker may either try to recall all of the plays after the ball is put down or write as play proceeds.

Shorthand Notation of Plays

Figure 7-11 adds tabular forms and scoring areas to the combined sideout-transition chart blank. The form for transition does not have space for ranking a pass since that is relevant only in serve

Figure 7-11: Adding Forms for Noting Plays and Scores

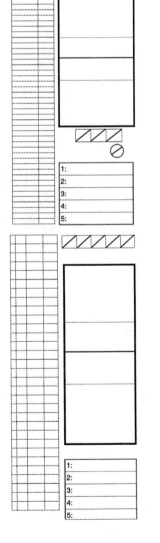

receive. The two columns are used to note the set and the score, if it changes at the end of the rally. If the team being charted scores a point, make a tally in the area below the transition chart. The column for the set is very versatile. The space may be used to note points scored by means other than a successful attack. A team may score by the block or by an opponent's hitting error. There are infinite ways to make a shorthand notation of this in the "set" column and add the score accordingly.

For example, Holland evened the score at 1-1 in game No. 3 when Zwerver put away a high ball on the left side hard cross-court. This would be noted in the transition form as:

h 8 +	1 - 1

Several rotations later, down 11-12, Holland blocked the Italian right-side hitter to tie at 12-12. This might be noted as:

2blk rsh	12 - 12

The particular form of shorthand is not important, but keeping track of how a team scores points can be vital to preventing them from doing so in the future.

Figure 7-12 shows a rally in game No. 4 with Italy up, 2-0. Swing hitter Bernardi (No. 9) serves; the ball is passed

Figure 7-12: The Transition Form to Record Plays While on Serve

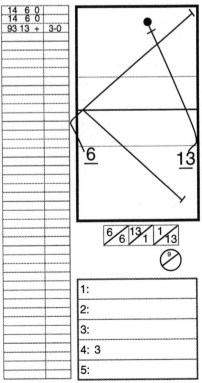

by van de Goor (No. 9); set quick by Blange (No. 12) to Held (No. 3), whose attack is touched and played up. Samuele Papi (No. 6), who came in for Cantagalli (No. 10) in the middle of the first game, hits hard cross-court from the left side, off the block, allowing Holland to dig and set van der Meulen (No. 11) on the right side. He goes off the block of Tofoli (No. 5) in area 1, who punches the ball up with one hand back to area 3. Andrea Gardini (No. 1) backsets Papi high; the Dutch block forces the attack back at Italy. Tofoli makes another great dig, again to Gardini, who now sets a 93 to Giani (No. 13), who crushes the ball off the block of Held and Zwerver (No. 8). Italy goes up, 3-0. Note that the bottom court is not used at all. All of the Italian hits described above are recorded on the transition chart; the third point is noted in the space below the chart in the area reserved for game No. 4.

The transition chart may also be entered during a rally in which the team being charted is receiving serve. That is, when the first attack does not result in a termination. In this case, the team may potentially lose a point. Although the transition plays need to be diagrammed on the top chart, any points lost should be noted in the space below the serve receive court. Particularly good point scoring rotations may then be identified, as well as particularly bad serve receive rotations.

Figure 7-13 puts all of the elements together. It shows Holland's rotation No. 3 (setter in left back) in the first three games. Both serve receive and transition are included with passing rankings, sets and scoring. Combination plays are clearly noted, as are high balls and off-speed shots. The transition set column contains not only attacks by Holland, but also its blocks of Italy and reception lapses by Italy. Two final elements complete the example: Underlining a point to represent an ace (see Holland's points allowed in game No. 3) and the marking "so" to indicate that a dug ball eventually led to a side-out.

Match Notes

The shorthand introduced in this

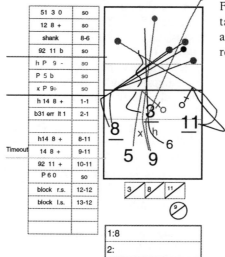

Figure 7-13: Holland's Rotation No. 3 After Three Games

(Note: The author is indebted to Fred Sturm for teaching him how to take a hitting chart and to Andy Read and Mark Pavlik for their critical readings of the manuscript.)

chapter is not a substitute for narrative. A good chart blank should have some space reserved for notes. Use this area to write down starters, substitutions, comments on the quality of play and even running scores, all of which is possible after a few matches of practice with the other components.

The Finished Product

The result of this construction project is shown at 75 percent scale in Figure 7-14. (The actual form is printed on legal-sized paper to ensure legibility.)

Figure 7-14: The Completed Chart Blank (75% Scale)

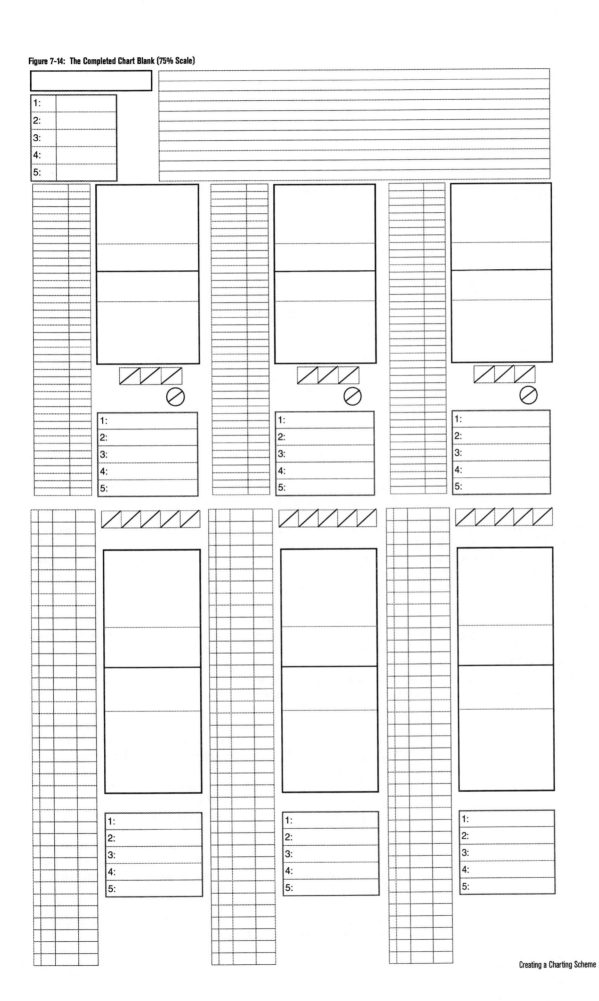

The Coach's Chart

The preceding section illustrated how to make a chart based on specific goals. The scheme developed has its strengths and some particular weaknesses. The astute reader will have noticed that the author has played fast and loose with the terms "set" and "play." In the charts shown previously, the author has typically recorded what set was hit by the attacker and the result. Volleyball offenses, however, revolve around plays — packages of options from which the setter attempts to find and set the one with the best chance of beating the defense. Coaches are, therefore, equally interested in knowing what all of the available hitters were doing. They ask, "What options did the offense show and which one did the setter choose?" For example, what positions were the left-side and opposite hitters running to when the middle hitter got the set? Did the offense show a middle shoot/left-side combination pattern before the setter went to the back-row attacker? Did the first or second hitter on an "x" get the ball?

This requires more space to record all of the relevant information. One very common implementation is to go the exact opposite route of the simple chart blank with which the journey began (Figure 7-1) to devote one full page per rotation and to sacrifice recording transition plays. Consider Figure 7-15 (page 77), which shows the chart blank used by the Penn State University's men's volleyball team. The rotation "pie" and large court for diagrams are self-explanatory. Therefore, let us focus on the large tabular form.

Using this chart requires being able to find hitters and diagram plays as discussed previously. The first 11 columns are shown in Table 3.

Filling in this table requires the

Table 4

Heading	Fill With
RSLT	K#: Kill to specified area (1 to 6)
	A or N: Error into antenna or net
	L# or W#: Error long or wide to specified area
	T#: Tip to specified area; add K if a kill results
	#: Area where ball is dug
	BB: Ball blocked back
	BD: Ball blocked down
BLK	Number of blockers up on the attack (0 to 3)

Table 5

Heading	Point Scored By
SRV	Service ace or winner
ATK	Attack
BLK	Block
OAE	Opponent's attack error (long or wide)
VIO	Violation (antenna, net, blockers in net, red card...)

ability to watch the entire court and see what all of the hitters are up to. This may be difficult initially, as the chart-taker develops his/her peripheral vision.

The remaining columns are found in Table 4. Recall that the naming convention for rotations is exactly opposite of that for defining the areas of the court. Rotation No. 3 refers to the setter being left back; area 3, however, is middle front.

Once a row is filled with the various options and the result is recorded, the hitter who got the set is circled. The three-row, seven-column table in the lower right corner is used to track scoring information. A tally mark is placed in the relevant cell whenever the team being charted or its opponent scores by one of the methods in Table 5.

Table 6

TO	SE	Score 2-0	# 9	GR 3	(SW) 82	M b61	OP 12	S	BS	BM	RSLT 5	Blk 2

Example

Early in game No. 2, Holland served in its rotation No. 3 (Blange left back) against Italy's rotation 1 (Tofoli right back). The front-row swing hitter, Bernardi (No. 9), passed the serve perfectly. Giani (No. 3) showed an approach for a 12 set; Gardini (No. 1) went behind Tofoli for a 61; Bernardi hit an 82 down the line against a double block on an inside-out approach and was dug in area 5 by Gortzen (No. 5). The row is filled as seen in Table 6.

The purpose of recording this information is to look for correlations between the tempo and position of the quick attacker and those of the outside attackers. It is a simple matter to determine what the quick hitter is doing; his approach is first tempo virtually by definition. The outsides are a little more tricky. They can come in at first, second or third tempo, depending on the pass and the quality of the setter. If one of the outside hitters gets set, note the set that he hit. If, however, the quick attacker gets set, make a reasonable guess at what the outside hitter was doing.

Figure 7-16 (page 79) depicts Italy's rotation No. 1 in the first game using the one-page-per-rotation chart. The roster is given in Table 7 (page 78).

Conclusion

Some examples of how to create charts have been shown, balancing the volume of data recorded with space available. At the time of this writing, a number of products can be used to create simple graphical and tabular forms. The effort comes in determining what information is required and in designing a procedure to obtain it in a timely, efficient and compact manner. To paraphrase the Cheshire Cat, "If you don't know where you are going, any road will take you there."

It is easy to get immersed in the specifics of charting while losing perspective. Any completed chart will usually need to be distilled and processed in order to be

Table 3

Heading	Explanation	Fill With
TO	Time-out	Check mark as required
SE	Opponent's service error	Check mark as required
Score		Score prior to contact of the ball for service
#	Jersey number of passer	
GR	Pass grade	0 to 3
SW, M, OP	Front-row swing hitter, middle, opposite	Sets that these players are preparing to attack
S	Setter	Does the setter threaten to dump on two when in the front row?
BS, BM	Back-row swing hitter, back-row middle	Sets that these players are preparing to attack, if required.

ROTATION # ☐

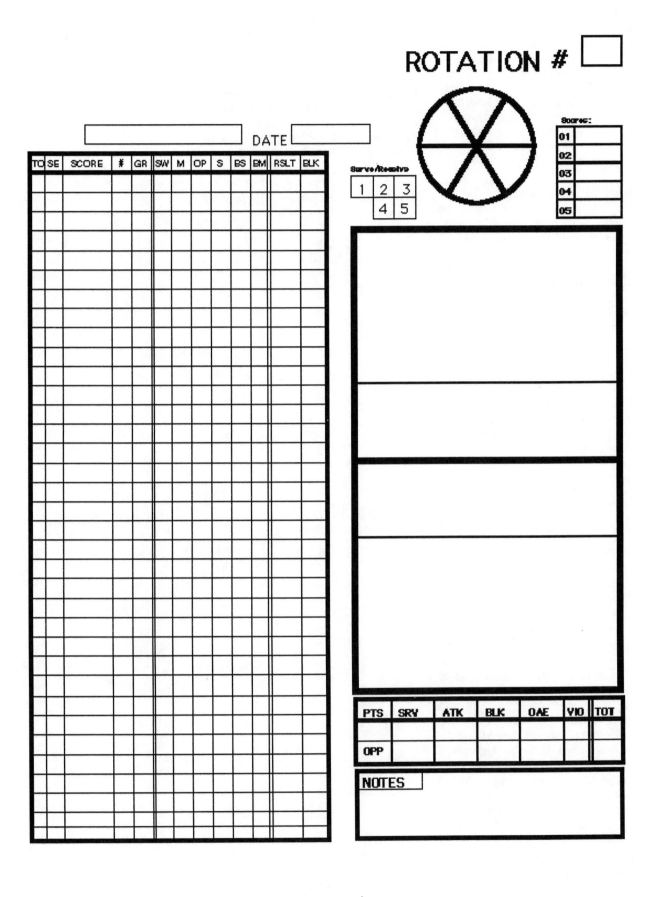

DATE ☐

Serve/Receive

1	2	3
	4	5

Score:

01	
02	
03	
04	
05	

TO	SE	SCORE	#	GR	SW	M	OP	S	BS	BM	RSLT	BLK

PTS	SRV	ATK	BLK	OAE	VIO	TOT
OPP						

NOTES

Table 7

Number	Name	Position
1	Andrea Gardini	Middle Blocker
3	Pasquale Gravina	Middle Blocker
10	Luca Cantagalli	Outside Hitter
6	Samuele Papi	Outside Hitter
9	Lorenzo Bernardi	Outside Hitter
13	Andrea Giani	Opposite
11	Andrea Zorzi	Opposite
2	Marco Meoni	Setter
5	Paolo Tofoli	Setter

digestible by players (e.g., Figure 5-6, page 48). The forest of lines in a raw chart must be replaced by a few concise indications of key hitters and their tendencies. A well-designed chart can show a match at a glance. It is, furthermore, a very economical way to record a match. The only investment is for a clipboard, some paper and pens. Videotape, however, can show timing which is much harder to codify. The advantage of computerized charting may lie in future developments that allow timing information to be noted easily and quickly displayed on the screen, perhaps even as animations. Charting and videotape are, therefore, complementary. This is the vital and difficult process of turning raw data into information. And even when that is done, the hard part is finding a way to turn that information into results.

The complete chart of the five-game 1996 men's Olympic gold medal match shows, for example, that Dutch opposite van der Meulen (No. 11) took a highly angled approach from the right side and hit hard cross-court from the front row. He did this from the left side, as well. He came in relatively straight from the D zone in the back row and tried to hit the seam between the blockers. This was doubtless known to the Italian coaches and players.

Late in game No. 3, Richard Schuil (No. 6) came in to serve for van de Goor (No. 9). Holland was down, 7-11, and Schuil's tough serves brought his team back to 9-11. He then served Papi (No. 6), whose pass at the 3-meter line allowed Tofoli (No. 5) to set Bernardi (No. 9) on the right side. This was promptly blocked back to Italy's area 1, where Tofoli made a tumbling dig to area 3. Gardini (No. 1) backset Giani (No. 13), who hit high hands off the block of van der Meulen (No. 11) and Held (No. 3). Zwerver (No. 8) made an equivalent dig of his own in area 4, high and to midcourt. Blange (No. 12) faced the net and flicked a front-row

right side ball to van der Meulen. Italy's defenders set up well — four diggers in a crescent — Giani ceded the line on the outside block, as he should have. Gardini was on his shoulder sealing off the seam perfectly. The heads of both were well above the net, their arms piked. van der Meulen simply took his approach, drove the ball well inside the block and neatly knocked Tofoli onto his back after hitting him squarely on the jaw.

Statistics or no statistics, the players ultimately must perform. Holland went on to take the match, 15-12, 9-15, 16-14, 9-15, 17-15.

TO	SE	SCORE	#	GR	SW	M	OP	S	BS	BM	RSLT	BLK
		0-0	10	1	(h9)	31	13				T4	0
		0-1	10	3	(93)	31	13				5	2
		2-1	10	0								
		2-2	9	3	(93)	b61	13			P	5	1
		2-3		3	93	(51)	13			P	K4	2
		5-3	10	3	92	b61	(12)				K5	2
		6-7	10	3	(93)	b61	13			P	KB	1
		8-11	9	3		(31)				P	K1	2
		10-12	6	3	(93)	51	13			P	K5	2
		11-13	9	3	93	(31)	13				K5	2

DATE

Serve/Receive

1	2	3
4	5	

Score:

01	
02	
03	
04	
05	

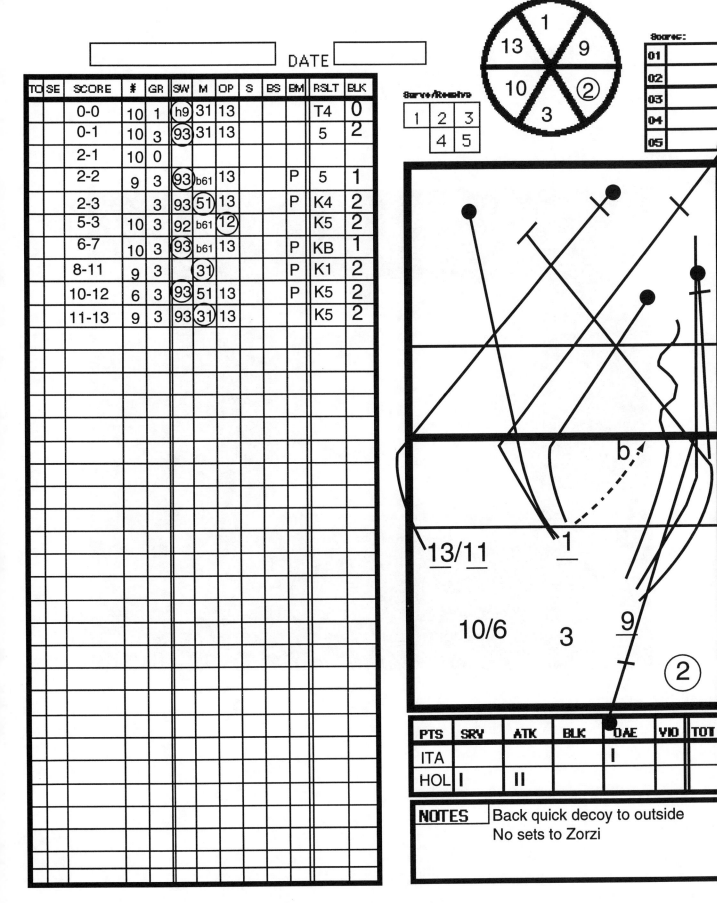

13/11

10/6   3   9

1

②

PTS	SRV	ATK	BLK	DAE	VIO	TOT
ITA				I		
HOL	I	II				

NOTES Back quick decoy to outside
No sets to Zorzi

Chapter 8

"The world is full of cactus, but we don't have to sit on it."
Will Foley

Computerized Statistics Software

It is a challenge for the modern-day coach to make use of available computer technology without losing focus of primary responsibilities—teaching, interacting with and leading athletes on a human level. A computer can analyze data; however, a computer cannot unlock the keys to success—having skills and those intangibles which allow a team to rise to the top. Competitive spirit, teamwork, discipline, trust, determination, motivation and integrity cannot be measured by a computer. A coach should not lose sight of the importance of those intangible human qualities which lead to success.

All things being equal, a coach armed with a computer print-out is not nearly as valuable to a team as a coach who understands how to lead people. It is dangerous for a coach to underestimate the impact of positive leadership. Computer statistics might diagnose a problem area, but a computer cannot fix the problem. It takes a coach, not a computer, to know how to affect positive change while making subtle modifications within the framework of a team. Computers are no panacea leading to success on the volleyball court.

Computers and software can also take a chunk out of a budget, which may already be limited. Coaches should consider putting limited available resources into people rather than computers.

Finally, coaches should be cautioned about making major decisions regarding team play with averages from a small number of entries. Small amounts of data (e.g., statistics from one game or match) can be misleading. Generally, 30 to 40 entries are needed to ensure some validity. With these cautionary thoughts in place, let us examine how computerized statistics programs can assist today's coach.

A thorough analysis of volleyball statistics once depended on the coach's or statistician's ability to sift through the recorded data. Early computer spreadsheets used to enter data were often cumbersome and filled with data which still had to be analyzed by an individual. Now it is possible to record and analyze volleyball statistics with the aid of a computer. In today's "computer age," many software programs have been developed to take the place of these older systems. The U.S. national teams have led the way in developing software to enhance the coach's ability to have real-time statistics available on the bench. Post-match analysis of data can now be accomplished with a few key strokes to the computer. For those with the financial resources and the technical knowledge to run computerized programs, the ease and reliability of the computer can provide the coach with an added edge. Coaches using computerized programs have almost instantaneous access to a wide variety of analytical data about the match in progress. Many of these schools have software programs used after the match where data is entered and compiled. This is not to say that the statistician on the bench with a clipboard is a thing of the past. Quite to the contrary, a large percentage of schools and junior programs still rely on hand-written data. In fact, many of the best coaches still prefer to take their own handwritten statistics from the bench.

In addition to having statistics available during competition to assist in making performance evaluations, computer statistical programs can be immensely helpful to the coach after the match. Analytical programs can guide the coach in planning practice sessions. For example, a software package can analyze the team's rotational productivity and immediately produce a print-out showing any weaknesses. With this information, the coach can either work on specific rotations to enhance the point scoring productivity or possibly work to improve the defense against the opponents. Perhaps the coach notes a weakness in only one serve re-ception rotation (side-out offense), suggesting a need to work on that specific rotation in practice. The possibilities for making the statistical analysis part of the practice plan are endless.

The purpose of this chapter is to present various types of software programs which are available. Because software technology changes so rapidly, specific programs will not be discussed. (Current information about individual software programs is available on the USAV website at http://www.volleyball.org.) One program will not be recommended over another; rather, the option will be presented and then you must select the software which best fits your program. The software programs can be divided into three categories: Media relations statistics, coaching statistics and organizational programs to assist coaches in everyday activities.

Media Relations Software

Media relations software provides information about a team or match that can be widely used by the media or sports information offices. Game statistics, box scores, play-by-play synopses and cumulative team and individual statistics reports are common pieces of information which can be gleaned from the media relations software. This type of software does not generally provide a coach with statistical analysis of the data. Look for capabilities to perform some or all of these functions in the media software:

•Individual and team match statistics - Some programs can provide these reports at courtside in real time and others must be entered following a match.

•Cumulative individual and team statistical reports as the season progresses - Some schools require NCAA or NAIA formats (or others for high schools) which are sent to conference or national offices. These are often used to select player-of-the-week honors or to compile lists of statistical leaders (team and individual) in specific skills.

•Box Score reports - Some programs will automatically compile a box score format at the end of a match.

•Play-by-play reports - Some programs incorporate this feature and will print out game and match terminal play actions for every point scored.

•Season, conference and non-conference totals - Reports can be printed for both the team and individuals for these areas in selected skills.

•"Quick stats" - Allows the operator to print out a report at any time during the match for team and individual leaders in selected categories.

•Faxing to media outlets - The program is capable of connecting directly into the files of media outlets. Some programs can even transmit an AP (Associated Press) short box score.

•Internet HTML ready - The program can be used to put information directly onto the Internet.

•Scoreboard interface - Some programs are designed to be ready to connect directly into an interface board, which can transmit statistics directly onto the arena scoreboard during a match.

Coaching Statistical Software

Software used specifically for coaching supplies statistics and analysis for a wide variety of individual and team skills. The reports provide data which can assist the coach in diagnosing problems for almost every aspect of the game. Many of the programs allow the computer operator to rate skill performance to enhance the analysis further. Analysis can vary from the most basic parts of the game (e.g., passing, serving and hitting) to more advanced analysis of productivity of the offense by rotation. Listed below are some of the capabilities of specific coaching software.

•Real-time statistics - Gives immediate feedback of data and analysis at any point during the input process. For example, after one game a coach could get a report showing what happened in the first game.

•Skill analysis - Allows the computer operator to use rating scales of 0 to 2 (usually "-", "0" and "+") to classify six basic skills: serve, pass, set, attack, block and dig. The ratings are usually based on the outcome of the play to maintain objectivity. Analysis includes totals for individuals and the team with comparisons from

game to game or match to match.

•Advanced skill analysis - Uses a rating scale of 0 to 4 to classify the performance of the six basic skills: serve, pass, set, attack, block and dig. The rating scale is based on the outcome of the action. The advanced skill analysis provides greater differentiation of skill performance. (Some programs do not divide blocking into four rankings.)

•Rotational analysis - Provides the coach with detailed reports of "points scored" and "points scored against" in each rotation during a game. Cumulative game and match totals are analyzed, pointing out positives and negatives in each rotation. This allows the coach to examine the productivity of the offense and the effectiveness of the defense.

•Extended analysis of skills - Allows the coach to subdivide several skills even further. For example, a coach could divide serving into serving from a certain area or serving with a jump serve. The report analyzes the effectiveness of one against the other.

•Set and/or setter analysis - Shows the setter's tendencies from different types of passes and digs. The program can show which sets work best for the team and for specific players.

•Advanced blocking analysis - Allows the coach to chart and record the effectiveness of specific blockers and for team blocking tactics.

•Side-out and point scoring analysis - Allows the coach to track the effectiveness of the team side-out offense and transition offense. Some programs will perform this function by rotation.

•Combination analysis - These programs can combine several skills or actions of several players to give an analysis of how their actions influence the team's success.

•Graphical analysis - Provides the coach with graphs and curves showing the relationship of skill performance to success. Some of these graphs show specific relationships such as how the zone of the set affects the attack percentages. More advanced programs can offer forecasts for the coach to use in planning a successful strategy.

•Cumulative totals - most software programs allow the coach to receive cumulative statistics from any of the functions performed by the program. This allows the coach to compile year-to-date totals over the course of a season.

•Game charting - Special technology now allows the coach to chart (with diagrams) the course of a match. Attack charts, serve reception charts and blocking charts can be drawn on the computer screen with a special pen.

Organizational Software

Organizational software can help make a coach's everyday tasks more efficient and thorough. Whether it is planning practice, scheduling, recruiting or budget tracking, these programs provide a way for the coach to handle daily life effectively. College coaches should especially appreciate the assistance a computer program can have in recruiting and rule compliance. Programs are available for:

•Practice scheduling - Plan and organize a practice session or a season. Calendars are included with some programs.

•Recruiting - Provide coaches with a means to evaluate, rank and track prospects. These programs can also create mailing lists and sort/merge lists for periodic letters.

•Compliance - Programs provide a means for tracking contacts, visits, evaluations and phone contacts. Collegiate coaches will find this helpful for data which is necessary for rule compliance regulations.

•Scheduling - Both conference and individual scheduling and tournament scheduling programs are available. Use this technology to do scheduling for virtually any league, school or junior program.

•Equipment management - Ideal for tracking the use of equipment for a program and helps to remind the coach when it is time to order new equipment.

•Expenses and budgets - Useful in writing expense reports and budget control.

•Player information - These databases can keep personal, academic, athletic and injury information about the individuals on the team.

Considerations for Selecting Software
Computer Equipment

The type of software a coach orders should obviously be compatible with the computer equipment one has at his/her disposal. Check with the dealer to find out the exact specifications needed to run software. Software is usually designed for Macintosh or IBM compatible systems. Ask about memory requirements for the software. If you are in a position to buy a computer, ask the volleyball software dealers to give some suggestions. How you plan to use it will make a big difference in any recommendations from the experts.

Personnel to Run the Software

The coach should make a decision about how the software programs will be used. Different systems require differing levels of expertise to operate the programs. Will a staff member be running the program at courtside or will the data be entered after the match by a manager? How much knowledge of the game is necessary to run the computerized program? How many people are necessary? Any number of possibilities or options are available to the coach.

Select the Software Which Meets Your Needs

Some software is designed primarily for coaching statistics and others are designed to serve as media relations tools. Be sure to select the software which best fits your requirements. Coaches at higher levels of play may want both. A club coach may want the software which enhances his/her ability to be an effective coach. Most software dealers have detailed descriptions of software capabilities.

Cost

The cost of most software programs seems to be within a similar range. However, make sure that the basic program includes all of the features you need. Some programs require purchase of additional packages to get all of the data capabilities you desire. Add up the cost of all of the programs and then compare costs. As dealers upgrade their programs, some will offer newer versions at discounted prices to those already using the programs.

Appendices

PRACTICE PASS AND SERVE STATISTICS

Date _____

PLAYER	SERVING		TOTALS	AVE	PASSING		TOTALS	AVE

Key: Serve or Pass Efficiency Ave. = Sum of Ratings for Each Pass or Serve / Number of Attempts

Passing: 3 = perfect pass/all options, 2 = setter can't set middle, 1 = setter has only one option, 0 = rec. error

Serving: 4 = ace, 3 = pass leaves setter with one option, 2 = setter can't set middle, 1 = perfect pass, 0 = error

MATCH PASS AND SERVE STATISTICS

DATE: _____

GAME SCORES: _____

VS _____

OPPONENTS		GAME 1		GAME 2		GAME 3	
		1 2 3 4 5 6 7 8 9 10 11 12 13 14 15 16 17		1 2 3 4 5 6 7 8 9 10 11 12 13 14 15 16 17		1 2 3 4 5 6 7 8 9 10 11 12 13 14 15 16 17	
		1 2 3 4 5 6 7 8 9 10 11 12 13 14 15 16 17		1 2 3 4 5 6 7 8 9 10 11 12 13 14 15 16 17		1 2 3 4 5 6 7 8 9 10 11 12 13 14 15 16 17	
PLAYER	#SUBS	SERVING	PASSING	SERVING	PASSING	SERVING	PASSING
	1 2 3						
	1 2 3						
	1 2 3						
	1 2 3						
	1 2 3						
	1 2 3						
	1 2 3						
	1 2 3						
	1 2 3						
	1 2 3						
	1 2 3						
	1 2 3						
TIMEOUTS	1 2	1 2		1 2		1 2	
SUBSTITUTIONS	1 2 3 4 5 6 7 8 9 10 11 12			1 2 3 4 5 6 7 8 9 10 11 12		1 2 3 4 5 6 7 8 9 10 11 12	
TEAM TOTALS							
PER GAME							

MATCH TOTALS

VS

OPPONENTS

PLAYER	SERVING		PASSING	
	ACE / ER RATIO	EFF.	EFF.	PERCENT PERFECT

TOTALS

GAME 4

SERVING 1 2 3 4 5 6 7 8 9 10 11 12 13 14 15 16 17

PASSING 1 2 3 4 5 6 7 8 9 10 11 12 13 14 15 16 17

GAME 5

SERVING 1 2 3 4 5 6 7 8 9 10 11 12 13 14 15 16 17

PASSING 1 2 3 4 5 6 7 8 9 10 11 12 13 14 15 16 17

#SUBS

1 2 3

1 2 3

1 2 3

1 2 3

1 2 3

1 2 3

1 2 3

1 2 3

1 2 3

1 2 3

1 2 3

1 2 3

TIMEOUTS 1 2 3

SUBSTITUTIONS 1 1 2 3 4 5 6 7 8 9 10 11 12 2

TEAM TOTALS

PER GAME

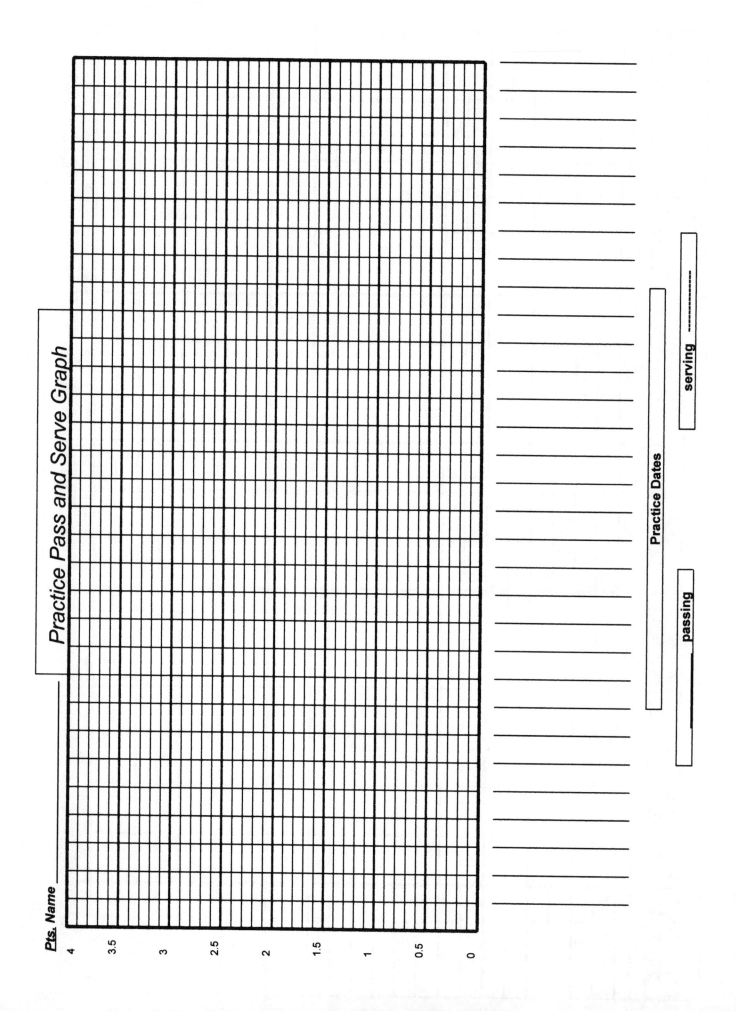

Practice Pass and Serve Graph

Pts. **Name** _____

4

3.5

3

2.5

2

1.5

1

0.5

0

Practice Dates

passing _____

serving - - - - - - - - - -

Name _____

INDIVIDUAL PASS AND SERVE

Date	Opponent	W / L	Site	PASSING				SERVING			
				Goal	Actual	%Perfect	Errors	Goal	Actual	Aces	Errors	A/E Ratio
Averages												

SEASON PASS AND SERVE

Date	Opponent	W / L	Site	TEAM PASSING					TEAM SERVING				
				Goal	Actual	%Perfect	Errors	Goal	Actual	Aces	Errors	A/E Ratio	
Averages													

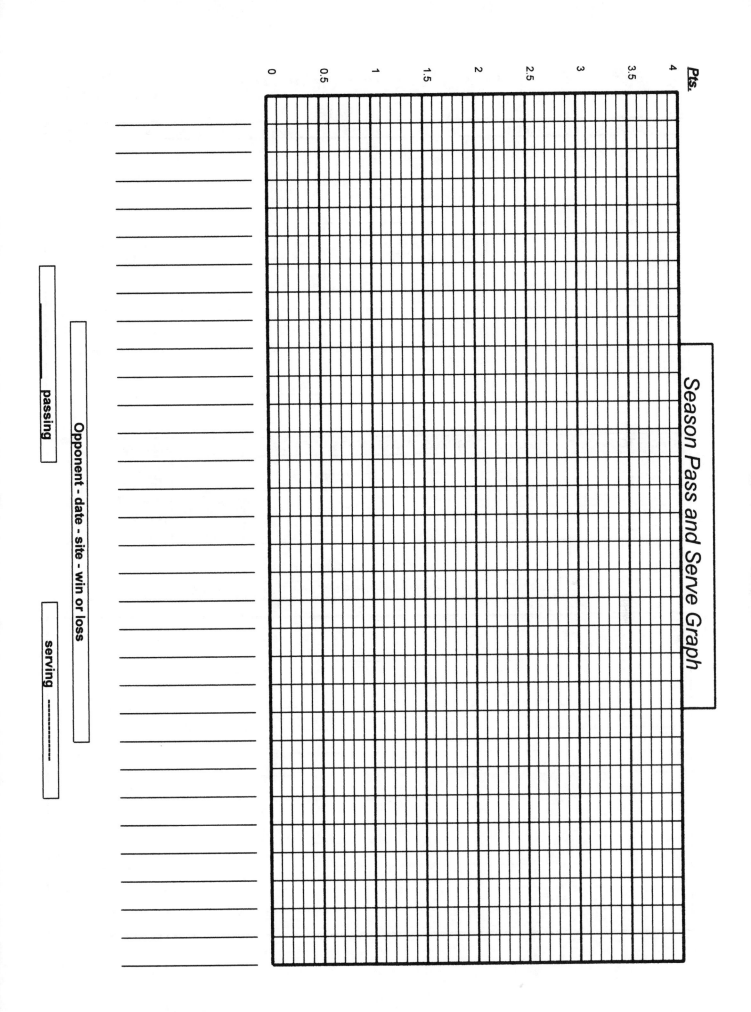

Season Pass and Serve Graph

Opponent - date - site - win or loss

passing

serving

Pts.

4

3.5

3

2.5

2

1.5

1

0.5

0

AVCA STATISTICS WORKSHEET

vs.   DATE: SITE:

PLAYER	NO	GAME 1	GAME 2	GAME 3	GAME 4	GAME 5	K	E	TA	PCT.

GAME TOTALS:	KILLS	ERRORS	ATTEMPTS	PCT.
1				
2				
3				
4				
5				

ATTACK KEY

0 = ATTACK ATTEMPT

● = KILL

∅ = ERROR

TA = 0 + ● + ∅

Pct. = (K - E) / TA

TO DISTINGUISH ONE GAME FROM ANOTHER USE DIFFERENT COLORED PENS

PLAYER	NO	ASSISTS	SA	SE	RE	DIGS	BS	BA	BE	BHE

ATTACK CHART

Team _____ **vs.** _____ **Date** _____

Player #___ Pos.___

Notes:

Player #___ Pos.___

Notes:

Player #___ Pos.___

Notes:

Player #___ Pos.___

Notes:

Player #___ Pos.___

Notes:

Player #___ Pos.___

Notes:

Player #___ Pos.___

Notes:

Player #___ Pos.___

Notes:

Player #___ Pos.___

Notes:

HITTING & BLOCKING CHART

vs _____ Date _____ Game # _____ Score _____

Rot. 1

player _____

BS	BA	BE
1	1	1
2	2	2
3	3	3
4	4	4
5	5	5
6	6	6
7	7	7
8	8	8
9	9	9
10	10	10

player _____

BS	BA	BE
1	1	1
2	2	2
3	3	3
4	4	4
5	5	5
6	6	6
7	7	7
8	8	8
9	9	9
10	10	10

Notes

player _____

BS	BA	BE
1	1	1
2	2	2
3	3	3
4	4	4
5	5	5
6	6	6
7	7	7
8	8	8
9	9	9
10	10	10

Rot. 2

player _____

BS	BA	BE
1	1	1
2	2	2
3	3	3
4	4	4
5	5	5
6	6	6
7	7	7
8	8	8
9	9	9
10	10	10

player _____

BS	BA	BE
1	1	1
2	2	2
3	3	3
4	4	4
5	5	5
6	6	6
7	7	7
8	8	8
9	9	9
10	10	10

Notes

player _____

BS	BA	BE
1	1	1
2	2	2
3	3	3
4	4	4
5	5	5
6	6	6
7	7	7
8	8	8
9	9	9
10	10	10

Rot. 3

player _____

BS	BA	BE
1	1	1
2	2	2
3	3	3
4	4	4
5	5	5
6	6	6
7	7	7
8	8	8
9	9	9
10	10	10

player _____

BS	BA	BE
1	1	1
2	2	2
3	3	3
4	4	4
5	5	5
6	6	6
7	7	7
8	8	8
9	9	9
10	10	10

Notes

player _____

BS	BA	BE
1	1	1
2	2	2
3	3	3
4	4	4
5	5	5
6	6	6
7	7	7
8	8	8
9	9	9
10	10	10

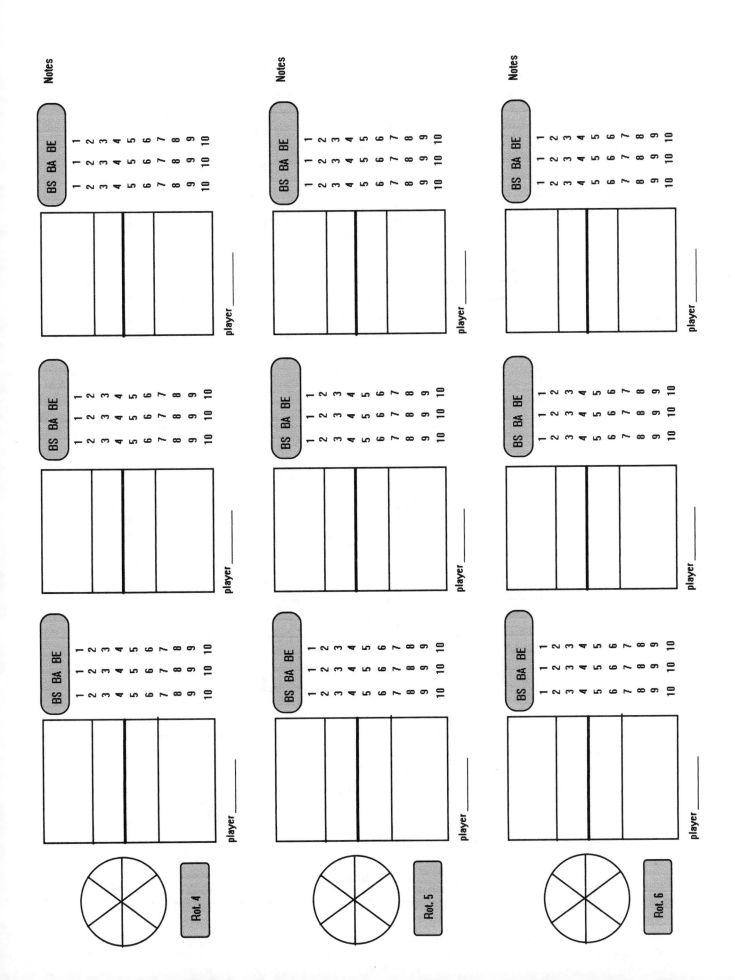

Set Selection Chart

Rotation 1

Pass	Set	Result									Notes
1.			11.			21.					
2.			12.			22.					
3.			13.			23.					
4.			14.			24.					
5.			15.			25.					
6.			16.			26.					
7.			17.			27.					
8.			18.			28.					
9.			19.			29.					
10.			20.			30.					

Rotation 2

Pass	Set	Result									Notes
1.			11.			21.					
2.			12.			22.					
3.			13.			23.					
4.			14.			24.					
5.			15.			25.					
6.			16.			26.					
7.			17.			27.					
8.			18.			28.					
9.			19.			29.					
10.			20.			30.					

Rotation 3

Pass	Set	Result									Notes
1.			11.			21.					
2.			12.			22.					
3.			13.			23.					
4.			14.			24.					
5.			15.			25.					
6.			16.			26.					
7.			17.			27.					
8.			18.			28.					
9.			19.			29.					
10.			20.			30.					

Key

Pass Ratings:
3 = all options (perfect pass)

2 = two options- no middle attack

1 = very limited options

X(#) = non-setter (player number)

Set Selection:
type/player #/rating

type = area & tempo (i.e., 31, 52)

rating :   + = good
0 = average
- = poor

Example: 72/3/+

Result:
K = kill
E = error
0 = dug
B = blocked/error
BHE = ball handling error
NE = net error
CE = centerline error

Rotation 4

Pass	Set	Result								Notes
1.			11.			21.				
2.			12.			22.				
3.			13.			23.				
4.			14.			24.				
5.			15.			25.				
6.			16.			26.				
7.			17.			27.				
8.			18.			28.				
9.			19.			29.				
10.			20.			30.				

Rotation 5

Pass	Set	Result								Notes
1.			11.			21.				
2.			12.			22.				
3.			13.			23.				
4.			14.			24.				
5.			15.			25.				
6.			16.			26.				
7.			17.			27.				
8.			18.			28.				
9.			19.			29.				
10.			20.			30.				

Rotation 6

Pass	Set	Result								Notes
1.			11.			21.				
2.			12.			22.				
3.			13.			23.				
4.			14.			24.				
5.			15.			25.				
6.			16.			26.				
7.			17.			27.				
8.			18.			28.				
9.			19.			29.				
10.			20.			30.				

Summary:

Rotation	Kills	Errors	0 Attacks	Best Hitter	Least Successful Hitter	Best Play	Comments
1							
2							
3							
4							
5							
6							

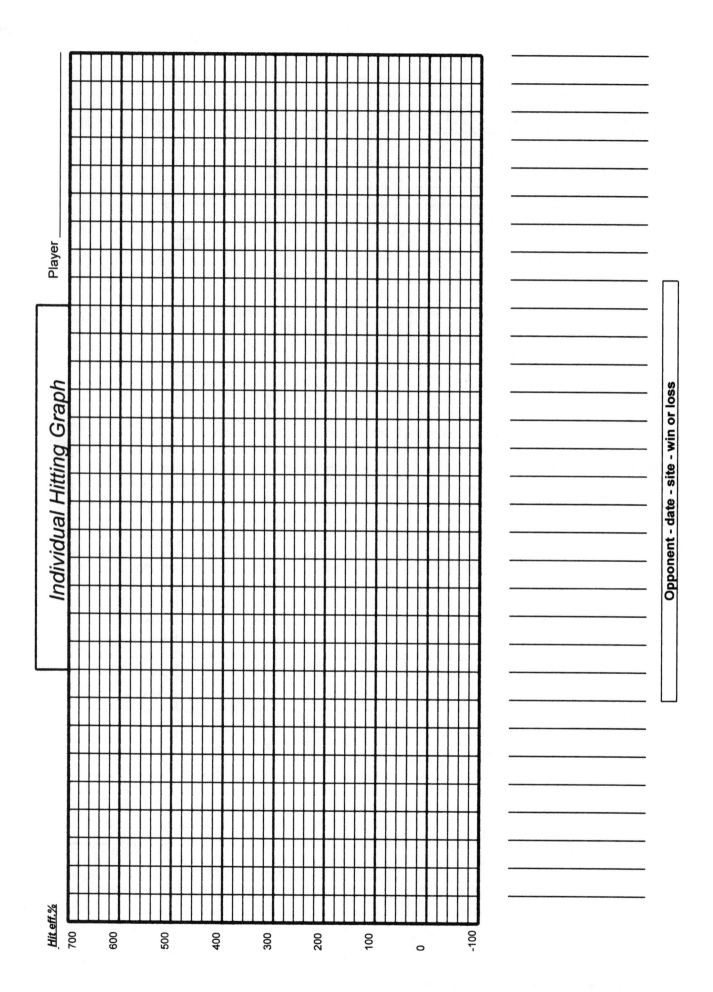

Individual Hitting Graph

Player _____

Hit eff.%

700
600
500
400
300
200
100
0
-100

Opponent - date - site - win or loss

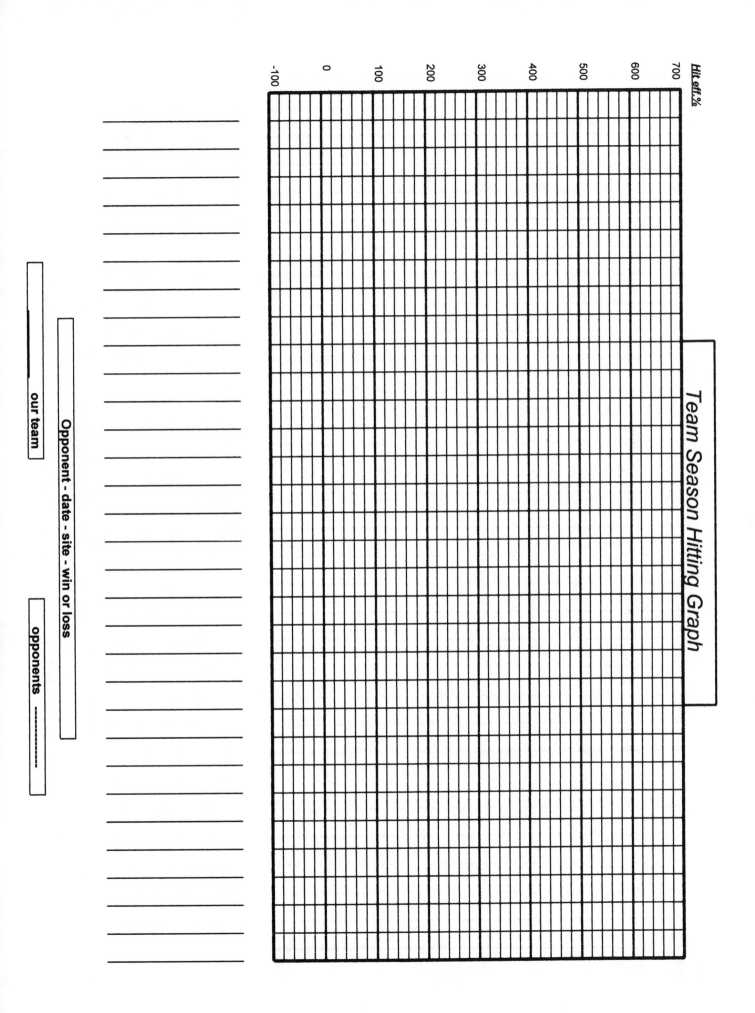

Team Season Hitting Graph

Hit eff.%

700 600 500 400 300 200 100 0 -100

Opponent - date - site - win or loss

our team

opponents

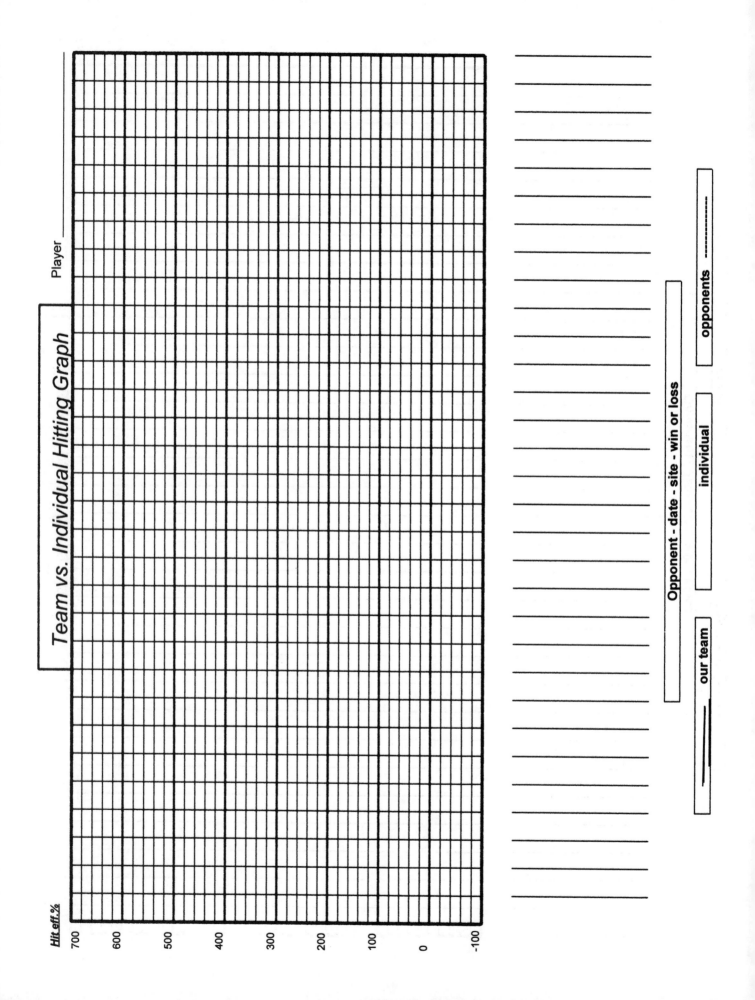

Team vs. Individual Hitting Graph

Player

Hit eff.%

700
600
500
400
300
200
100
0
-100

Opponent - date - site - win or loss

our team ──────

individual

opponents ┈┈┈┈┈┈

Name _____

INDIVIDUAL SUMMARY HITTING & BLOCKING

Date	Opponent	W / L	Site	BLOCKING					HITTING					
				Goal	B/GM	Total	Assist	Solo	Goal	Att.	Kills	Err.	Eff.	K %
Averages														

TEAM SUMMARY HITTING & BLOCKING

Team ____

Date	Opponent	W / L	Site	BLOCKING					HITTING					
				Goal	B/GM	Total	Assist	Solo	Goal	Att.	Kills	Err.	Eff.	K %
Averages														

OFFICIAL AVCA BOX SCORE

Site: Date: Attendance:

TEAM:

No.	Player	GP	ATTACK				SET	SERVE			DEF	BLOCK			GEN
			K	E	TA	PCT.	A	SA	SE	RE	DIG	BS	BA	BE	BHE

TEAM TOTALS:

Team Attack Per Game: Team RE: Total Team Blocks:

Gm	K	E	TA	Pct.	Pts	Game Scores	1	2	3	4	5	Team Records
1												
2												
3												
4												
5												

TEAM:

No.	Player	GP	ATTACK				SET	SERVE			DEF	BLOCK			GEN
			K	E	TA	PCT.	A	SA	SE	RE	DIG	BS	BA	BE	BHE

TEAM TOTALS:

Team Attack Per Game: Team RE: Total Team Blocks:

Gm	K	E	TA	Pct.	Pts	
1						Length of Match:
2						First Referee:
3						Second Referee:
4						Notes:
5						

Key:

A = Assists	GP = Games Played	BHE = Ball Handling Errors	SA = Service Ace	Kill Pct = (K - E) / TA
K = Kills	TA = Total Attempts	RE = Receiving Errors	SE = Service Error	D = Digs
E = Errors	Pct = %	SA = Block Solos	Team Blocks = BS + 1/2 BA	BE = Block Errors
		BA = Block Assists	Team RE = RE not assigned to any one player	

Points Per Rotation Summary

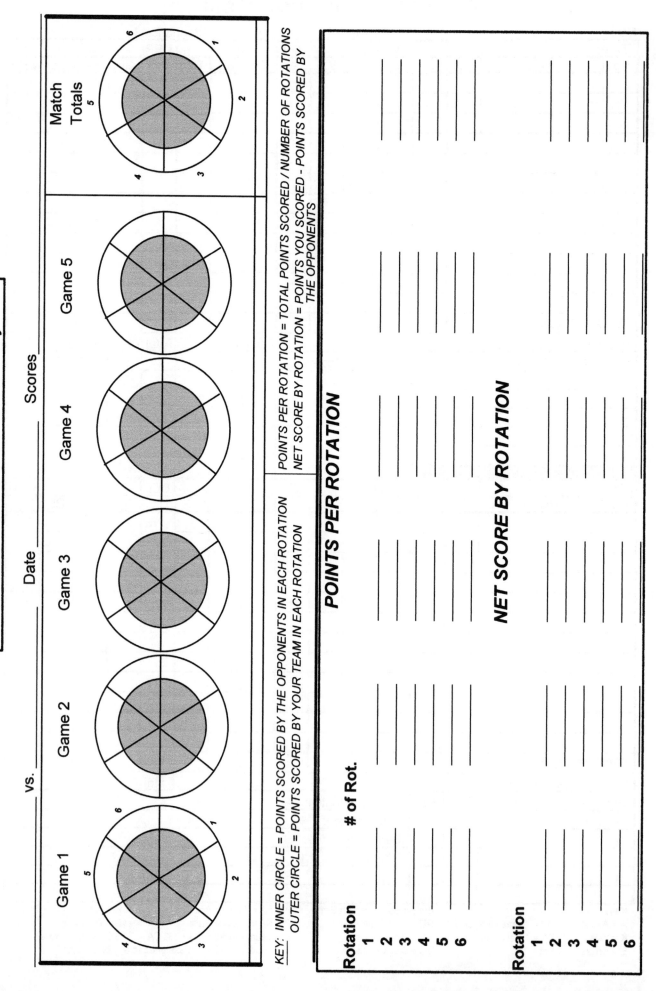

vs. _____

Date _____

Scores _____

| Game 1 | Game 2 | Game 3 | Game 4 | Game 5 | Match Totals |

KEY: INNER CIRCLE = POINTS SCORED BY THE OPPONENTS IN EACH ROTATION
OUTER CIRCLE = POINTS SCORED BY YOUR TEAM IN EACH ROTATION

POINTS PER ROTATION = TOTAL POINTS SCORED / NUMBER OF ROTATIONS
NET SCORE BY ROTATION = POINTS YOU SCORED - POINTS SCORED BY THE OPPONENTS

POINTS PER ROTATION

# of Rot.

Rotation
1
2
3
4
5
6

NET SCORE BY ROTATION

Rotation
1
2
3
4
5
6

SCOUTING CHART

Team _____ *Site* _____ *Date* _____

Starting Rotation: ____ *game 1,* ____ *game 2,* ____ *game 3,* ____ *game 4,* ____ *game 5*

Serve Receive   Transition

Rotation
1

Rotation
2

Rotation
3

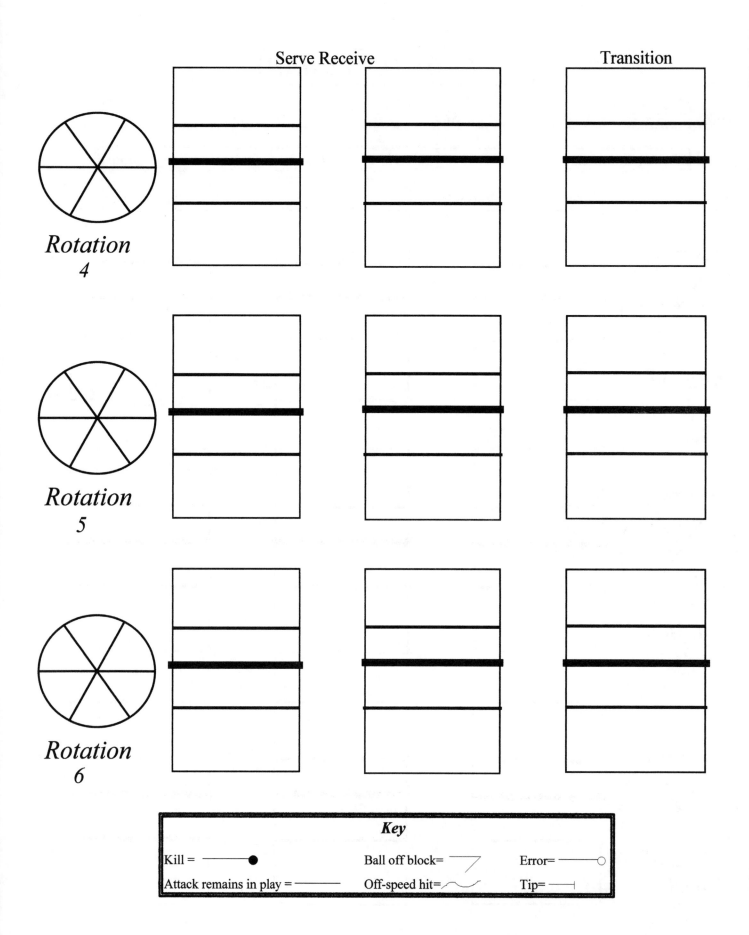

Serve Receive   Transition

Rotation
4

Rotation
5

Rotation
6

Key

Kill = ●

Ball off block = ⟍⟋

Error = ○

Attack remains in play = ————

Off-speed hit = ∿

Tip = ⊣

DEFENSE CHART

Team _____ *vs.* _____ *Date* _____

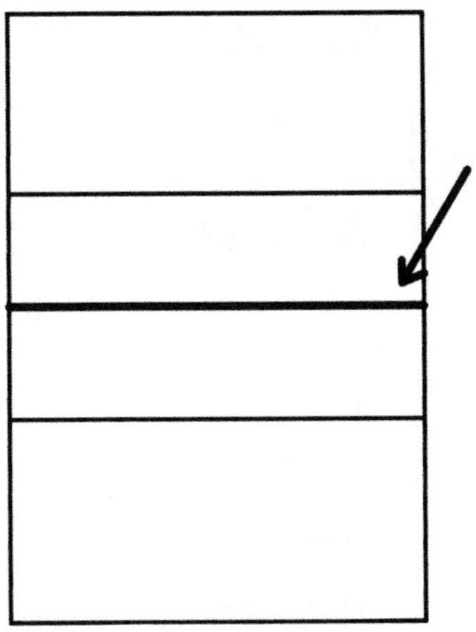

Attack from left side

Notes:

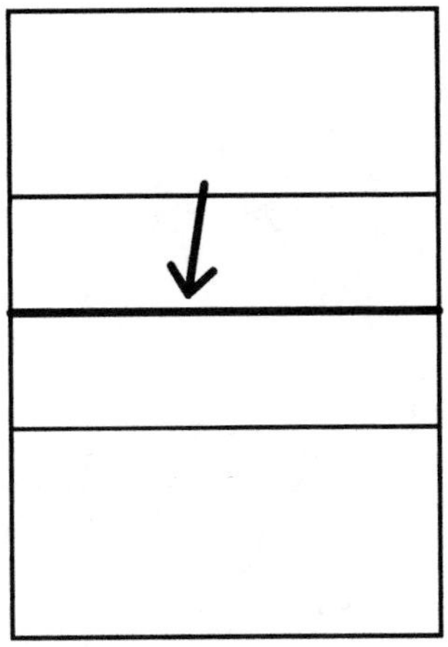

Attack from middle

Notes:

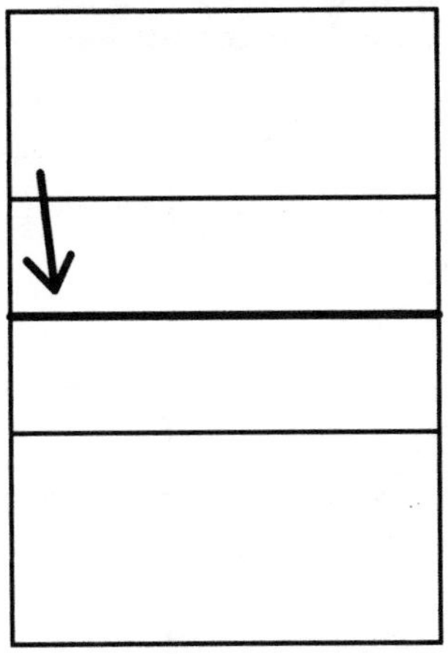

Attack from right

Notes:

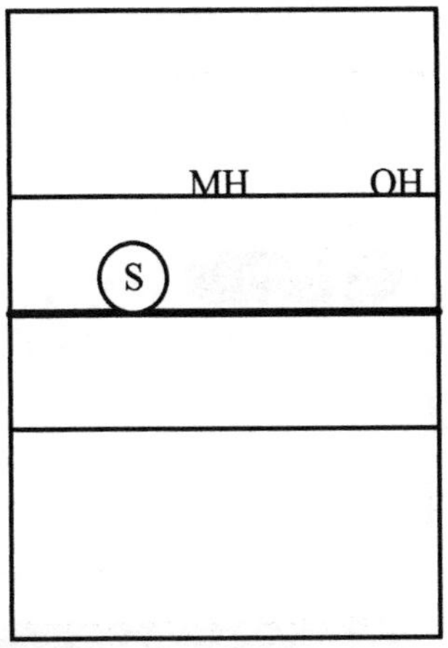

MH   OH

S

Base Position - S front row

Notes:

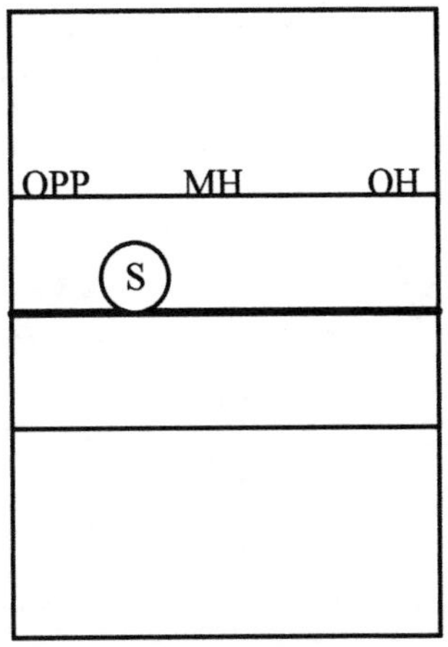

OPP   MH   OH

S

Base position - S back row

Notes:

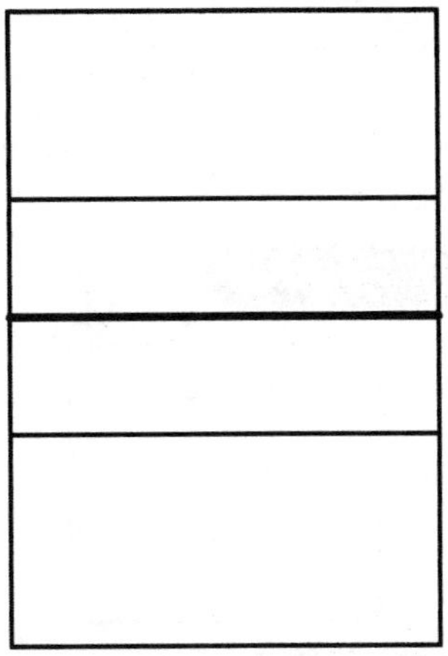

Back row attack

Notes:

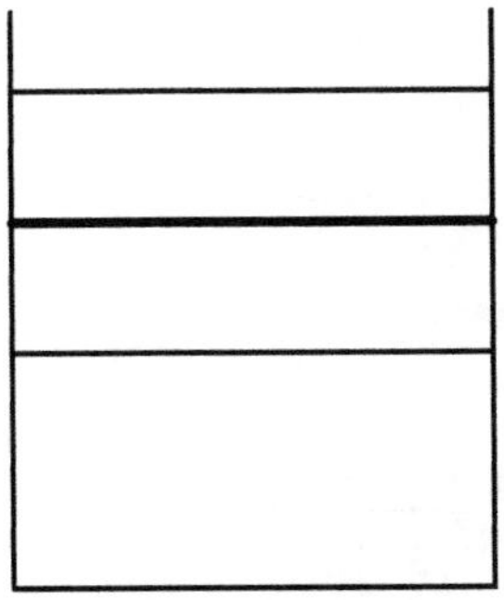

Combination plays

Notes:

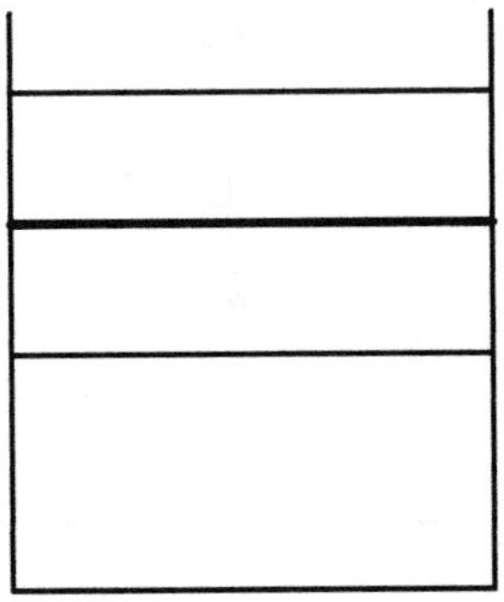

Combination plays

Notes:

Best Blocker(s): _____

Poor Blocker(s): _____

Middle Blocker Tendencies:

_____

_____

Defense vs. Slide: _____

_____

OPPONENT SNAPSHOT

Team_____

Serve Receive Offense

1.

2.

3.

4.

5.

6.

Offense

Line-up

S:_____

MH:_____

OH:_____

OPP:_____

Lefties:_____

Best Passers:

_____

Serving Targets

_____

_____

_____

Team Defense

Defense

Shot Charts

#__

#__

#__

#__

#__

#__

Hitting Tendencies

#_____

#_____

#_____

#_____

#_____

#_____

Notes

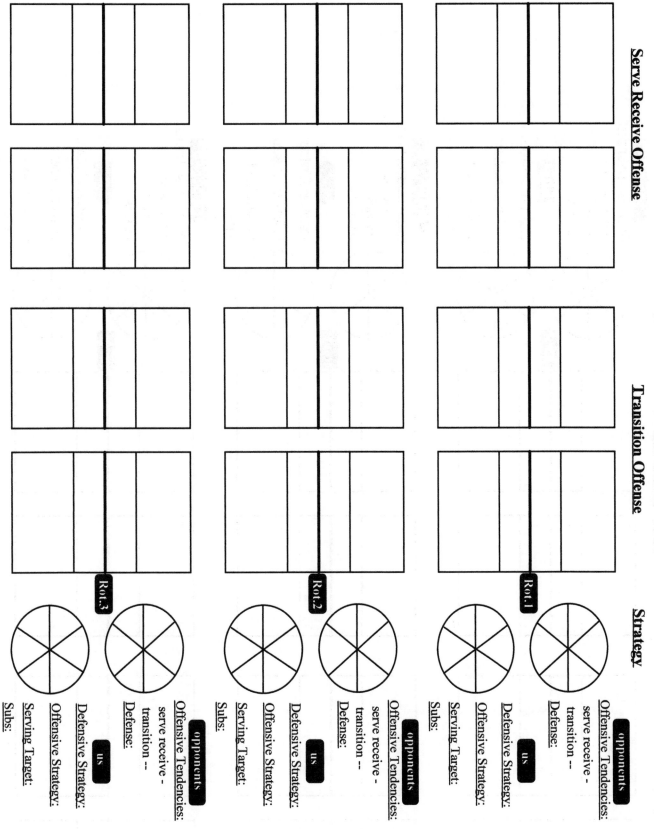

MATCH-UP CHART

Serve Receive Offense | Transition Offense | Strategy

Rot.3 | **Rot.2** | **Rot.1**

Rot.1 / opponents
Offensive Tendencies:
serve receive -
transition --
Defense:

us
Defensive Strategy:
Offensive Strategy:
Serving Target:
Subs:

Rot.2 / opponents
Offensive Tendencies:
serve receive -
transition --
Defense:

us
Defensive Strategy:
Offensive Strategy:
Serving Target:
Subs:

Rot.3 / opponents
Offensive Tendencies:
serve receive -
transition --
Defense:

us
Defensive Strategy:
Offensive Strategy:
Serving Target:
Subs:

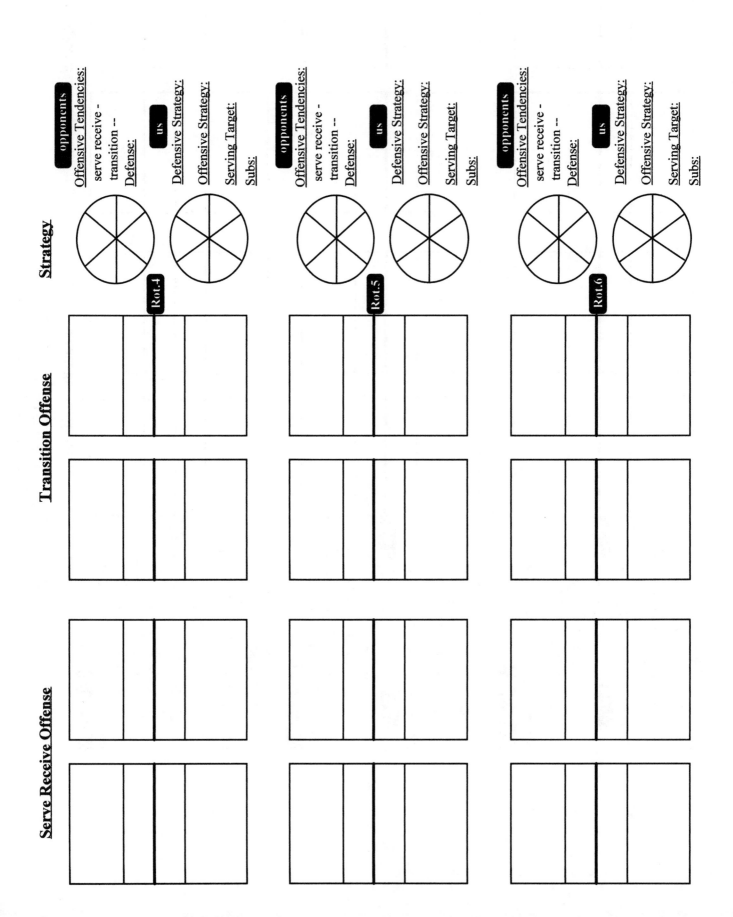

Strategy

Transition Offense

Serve Receive Offense

opponents
Offensive Tendencies:
serve receive -
transition --
Defense:

us
Defensive Strategy:
Offensive Strategy:
Serving Target:
Subs:

Rot.4

opponents
Offensive Tendencies:
serve receive -
transition --
Defense:

us
Defensive Strategy:
Offensive Strategy:
Serving Target:
Subs:

Rot.5

opponents
Offensive Tendencies:
serve receive -
transition --
Defense:

us
Defensive Strategy:
Offensive Strategy:
Serving Target:
Subs:

Rot.6

GAME PLAN

Team _____   **Date** _____

Key Players:

What do we need to do to win?

Blocking Strategy:

Serving Strategy:

Attacking Strategy:

POINT SCORING CHART

_____ VS._____   Game # _____   Date_____

Team: _____   **Team:** _____

Type of Play	Player #	Point Number	Type of Play	Player #
		1		
		2		
		3		
		4		
		5		
		6		
		7		
		8		
		9		
		10		
		11		
		12		
		13		
		14		
		15		
		16		
		17		
		18		
		19		
		20		
		21		
		22		
		23		
		24		
		25		
		26		
		27		
		28		
		29		
		30		

GAME SUMMARY

Points For

Type	# Points
Kill	
Ace	
Stuff Block	
Opponent Error	

Points Against

Type	#Points
Kill	
Ace	
Stuff Block	
Our Error	

Key

K = Kill	SB = Stuff Block	BHE = Ball Handling Error	O = Overlap Error
A = Ace	NV = Net Violation	SE = Service Error	AE = Attack Error

WEEKLY PRACTICE PLANNER

Date _____

Day	Primary Focus		Seconday Focus	
	Team	Individual	Team	Individual
Monday				
Tuesday				
Wednesday				
Thursday				
Friday				
Saturday				

Day	Notes and Special Announcements		

PRACTICE PLAN

Date _____ *Primary Focus* _____

Time   *Warm-Up*

Individual Skills

Positional/Group Work

Team Drills/Competition

Cool Down

Announcements

VOLLEYBALL TEAM

Date _____

Remember to Bring to Practice:

Remember to Do:

Announcements:

VOLLEYBALL CALENDAR

Month _____

Sunday	Monday	Tuesday	Wednesday	Thursday	Friday	Saturday

Date _____   Name _____

Player Conference Outline

Please complete this form before your scheduled conference.

1. How do you feel about your academic progress? What problems are you having?
What is your plan to deal with these?_____
_____
_____
_____
_____

2. Do you think your fitness level (cardiovascular, strength, and body weight) have an
effect on your volleyball skill and success? If so, how? If no, why not?_____
_____
_____
_____
_____

3. How did you feel about your physical condition (fitness) this past season? What
changes, if any, would you like to make?_____
_____
_____
_____
_____

4. How do you think the coaching staff can assist you in making changes or
improvements in your fitness level?_____
_____
_____
_____
_____

5. How did you feel about your role on the team this past season?_____
_____
_____
_____
_____

6. What do you project as your role for next year?_____
_____
_____
_____
_____

7. What do you need to do to help yourself fulfill the role you want? What is your plan?
List several specific steps:

        a. _____

        b. _____

        c. _____

        d. _____

        e. _____

8. Other things you would like to talk about. _____

_____

_____

_____

_____

Schneid's Volleyball Dictionary

Copyright ©1996 by Mike Schneider (used by permission). Special thanks to Jeff Lucas (author of *Pass, Set, Crush*), and Bill Neville, head women's volleyball coach at the University of Washington (and author of *Coaching Volleyball Successfully,* both available through Volleyball Informational Products at 1-800-275-8782) for granting Schneid, Schleuder and VIP the permission to use definitions from their books to compose this dictionary.

3-meter line
    n. the attack line.

31X
    n. a series of plays in which the middle attacks the three (31) and the left crosses, fake-crosses or flairs from the three-hitter.

51X
    n. a series of plays in which the middle attacks the one (51) and the right crosses, fake-crosses or flairs from the one-hitter.

4-2
    n. an offense with four spikers and two setters. The setters are setters when they are in the front row and defenders when they are in the back row.

5-1
    n. an offense with five spikers and one setter.

6-2
    n. an offense with four spikers and two setters. The setters are spikers when they are in the front row and setters when they are in the back row.

10-foot line
    n. the attack line. A slight misnomer since the line is actually 3 meters from the center line.

ace
    n. a service ace.

angle
    n., adj. cross-court.

antenna
    n. a flexible rod that rises above the net to delineate the sideline boundary. The antenna is considered part of the net and is out-of-bounds.

assist
    n. awarded when a player passes, sets or digs the ball to a teammate, who attacks the ball for a kill.

attack
    n. the attempt by one team to terminate the play by hitting the ball to the floor on the opponent's side. The term refers to an individual effort or a combined team offensive pattern.

attack angle
    n. the direction of a spiker's approach to a set ball and the imaginary path of the spike across the net if hit in the same line as the approach angle.

attack approach
    n. the accelerating running movement of a spiker, usually involving three or four steps, to the point where the spiker jumps to hit the ball.

attack error
    n. results when an attacker hits the ball out-of-bounds, is stuffed by the opposing blockers, hits the ball into the antenna, is called for an illegal contact, hits the ball down on his/her side of the net, touches the net or is called for a line violation.

attack percentage
    n. a statistic used to determine a player's or team's attack effectiveness, defined as (kills - attack errors)/attack attempts. A negative attack percentage is possible (if there are more errors than kills).

attacker
    n. A player who attempts to hit a ball offensively with the purpose of terminating the play in his/her team's favor.

attack line
    n. a line 3 meters from, and parallel to, the net. A back-row player cannot legally attack the ball above the net unless he/she takes off on the jump from behind this line. See also 10-foot line, 3-meter line.

audible
    n. a play called in mid-rally.

auxiliary setter
n. the player assigned to set when the designated setter cannot, usually the right-front player.

back one
n. a low, quick set behind the setter.

back row
n. the three players whose court position, according to the official scorekeeper, is near the baseline.

back set
n. a set delivered behind the setter.

back slide
n. a quick slide behind the setter.

backspin
n. the resulting movement of the ball when spin is imparted in the vertical plane in a backward direction, usually due to striking underneath the ball.

ball handling error
n. charged when a player is called for mishandling the ball (usually a lift or a double hit) while digging or setting.

baseline
n. the back boundary of the court. See also endline.

beach dig
n. an overhead dig characterized by using open hands, fingers straight but together, either with thumbs alongside each other or the front of one hand pressed against the back of the other hand. It is often executed with a pushing motion, considered illegal indoors but legal outdoors.

block
n. 1. the combination of one, two or three players jumping in front of the opposing spiker and contacting the spiked ball with the hands. v. 2. the action of stopping or slowing a spiked ball with the hands above the net.

block assist
n. awarded when two or three players block the ball into the opponent's court for a point or side-out. Each player receives a block assist even if only one player actually blocks the ball.

block attempt
n. the action of blocking without touching the ball.

block error
n. charged when the blocker touches the net or is called for a line violation, illegal contact, back-row block or reaching over the net.

block solo
n. awarded when one player blocks the ball into the opponent's court for a point or side-out. That player is the only blocker attempting to block the ball.

blocker(s)
n. the player(s) responsible for blocking the opponent's attack.

block shadow
n. the shadow of the block.

break
n. an abrupt change of direction in the attacker's approach.

break point
n. the spot where the attacker changes direction.

broad jump
n. a forward jump in the attacker's approach.

bump
n. descriptive slang term for forearm passing.

center line
n. the line which lies in the plane of the net and extends from sideline to sideline, dividing the court.

camel toe
n. a ball struck with knurled fingers.

chain of command
n. the levels of authority on the team.

cobra

n. a ball struck with straight, locked fingertips

collapse

n. a defensive posture where a defensive player sits over one heel while playing a ball and rolls on his/her back. Used to play balls close to the floor and to cushion hard spikes during retrieval attempts, this skill is also known as a half roll.

combination

n. an offensive play that includes two or more players who attack in concert.

commit

n. a blocking scheme in which one player, usually the middle blocker, jumps with, and attempts to stuff, the quick attacker.

complementary set

n. a medium-height set that combines with the quick set.

control block

n. a block attempt that deflects and slows down a spiked ball so the back-row defenders can easily play it.

counter-rotate

n. a back-ourt defense in which the off-blocker moves near the block and the middle back moves to the cross-court corner.

cover the hitter

v. to perform spike coverage.

creep

v. to move stealthily so as to escape notice.

cross

n. 1. a combination in which the path of one attacker crosses the path of another. 2. cross-court.

crossover

n. a lateral footwork pattern in which the second step crosses over the first; used to cover medium distances.

cross-court

n., adj. an individual attack directed at an angle from one end of the offensive team's side of the net to the opposite sideline of the defensive team's court.

cross step

n. a footwork pattern designed to allow a player to move quickly to a correct, balanced precontact position in either forearm or overhead passing.

deep

adj. away from the net, toward the endline.

defensive system

n. a team tactical system of deploying players to positions to defend against an opponent's attack. An effective system deploys players in the areas most likely to be attacked and takes the strengths and weaknesses of the individual defenders into account.

dig

n. 1. the act of retrieving an attacked ball close to the floor. 2. Awarded when a player successfully passes a ball which has been attacked by the opposition.

dink

n., v. slang for tip.

disappear

v. to position oneself behind a teammate attacker so as to be hidden from the blocker's view.

dive

n., v. a defensive retrieval technique in which a player extends for a ball near the floor, causing both feet to leave the floor. The player contacts the ball with one or both arms and slides on the abdomen and thighs.

double block

n., v. a block formed by two players.

double contact

n. contacting the ball twice in succession, or the ball contacts various parts of the body successively.

double hit

n. a double contact.

double-stack
n. a commit-block scheme in which both the left and the right start behind the middle in order to follow the crossing attacker.

down ball
n. an attack, neither a hard spike nor a free ball, usually made by a player with his/her feet on the floor, which the defense tries to field with its back-court players only.

dump
n. 1. a ball that has been attacked by the setter on the second contact-v. 2. to attack the ball on the second contact -interj. 3. an exclamation made by a player to inform his/her teammates that the setter is attacking the ball.

extension roll
n. a defensive retrieval technique similar to a dive, except that after contacting the ball with either one or two arms, the player turns as the body contacts the floor and rolls as the momentum of the movement carries the feet over the shoulder, returning the player to his or her feet.

fake cross
n. a play that starts as a cross but changes the direction of its play-set hitter with a veer.

fake X
n. a play in which the right fake-crosses the one-hitter and then attacks to the right of the setter.

five
n. a medium-height set on the right sideline.

flair
n. a play in which the right fake-crosses the one-hitter and then attacks on the right sideline.

float serve
n. a floater.

floater
n. a serve that moves in an unpredictable path due to lack of spin.

floor defense
n. any retrieval of an attacked ball that gets by the block.

follow
n. to move with, and then block, an attacker, often changing positions with another blocker in the process.

follower
n. the outside blocker who crosses the commit blocker.

forearm pass
n. one of the six basic volleyball skills. It is a ball-handling skill that a player uses to contact the ball legally at a level below the waist using the forearms as the contact surface. See also bump.

four
n. a shoot that is attacked near the left sideline.

free ball
n. 1. a slow, arcing shot, allowing an easy pass and a good attack by the receiving team. -interj. 2. an exclamation made by a player to inform his/her teammates that they will receive a free ball.

front
v. to position oneself, in order to block, in front of the attacker's arm.

front-row
n. the three players whose court position, according to the official scorekeeper, is near the net.

front slide
n. a quick slide in front of the setter.

gameplan
n. the team's offensive and defensive emphases for a particular opponent, usually organized by rotation.

glide
n. a long, smooth run that precedes a spike.

hit
n., v. spike.

hitter

n. an attacker.

hut

n. a medium-height set on the left sideline; the term originated from the hitter's mid-rally call to the setter.

inside

n. toward the center of the net.

inside the block

n. a ball that has been attacked in the cross-court angle so that it passes by the block nearest the center of the court.

J stroke

n. A modified forearm pass technique where the thumbs are turned up and the elbows are bent, forming a "J". This technique is used to dig hard-hit balls and balls played close to the net.

jump serve

n. a serve in which the player jumps and attacks the ball as in spiking.

jump set

n. a set executed while the setter is in the air.

junk

n. Slang for off-speed shots, balls intentionally hit off the block and deflected shots that do not travel in expected paths or to anticipated locations.

kill

n. an attacked ball that strikes the floor or lands out-of-bounds after touching an opponent.

kill efficiency

n. attack percentage.

knuckler

n. an emergency one-hand technique used to play a ball close to the face and tight to the net. The fingers are curled at the second knuckle and the hand is cocked back. The ball is actually contacted on the heel of the hand.

left-stack

n. a commit-block scheme in which the left starts behind the middle in order to follow the crossing attacker.

lift

n. an illegal contact resulting when the ball is in contact with the player for too long.

line shot

n. a straight-ahead, sideline attack.

lineup

n. the players' serving order, which reflects their starting locations on the court.

load

n. to arrange the blockers so that the team's most effective blocker confronts the opponents' most effective attacker.

middle

n. either the middle-front or middle-back player.

midline

n. an imaginary line drawn equidistant from the sidelines, that is, lengthwise, on the court; an imaginary line drawn vertically on the player's body that divides it into comparable left and right parts.

multiple-attack

n. an offense consisting of plays in which two or more players attack at different places on the net at different times.

net block

v. slang describing when a blocker places his/her hands, palms forward, against the net to deflect a ball that has been passed into the net by the opponents.

off-blocker

n. the outside blocker not included in the double block.

off-hand

n. a set delivered from the left side of the right-handed attacker and vice-versa.

off-speed shot
n. any ball spiked with less than maximum force but with spin. vice-versa.

on help
n. a player's defensive floor position and body posture that allows him/her to play an attacked ball in front of the body and toward teammates.

one
n. a low, quick set that is attacked either directly in front of or behind the setter.

one-footed slide
n. an approach to attack that includes a one-footed jump long the net.

on-hand
n. a set delivered from the right side of the right-handed spiker and vice-versa.

open-handed tip
n., v. tip.

open up
n. to step away from and face the ball's path in receiving serve.

opposite
n. three positions away in the line-up; the player opposite the setter.

outside
n. toward the sideline.

outside-in
n. defending, either at the net or in the back-court, from the sideline to the interior of the court.

overlap
n. a foul in which one player is out of position in relation to another player (defined by player's foot placement) when the ball is served.

overhead pass
n. a ball-handling skill using both hands simultaneously to contact the ball above the head and direct it to the intended target.

overpass
n. a ball that is passed across the net.

overset
n. a ball that is set across the net.

pace
n. the overall rhythm of the team or of a player.

pancake
n. a one-handed defensive technique in which the player flattens his/her hand against the floor in order to save the ball.

pass
n. the first contact of a served ball; a forearm pass.

pepper
n. a (usually) warm-up drill in which two players pass, set and hit the ball back and forth.

perimeter
n. a back-court defense in which four players arrange themselves near the boundaries of the court.

pike
n. to bend forward at the waist so that both the torso and the legs are in front of the hips.

play
n. an attack with a planned fake, usually including two or more hitters; a combination.

play-set
n. a medium-height set usually near the middle of the court that, when combined with a quick set, constitutes a play.

point
n. a front-row position in the serve-receive formation; the unit of scoring.

point of contact
n. the place on the court or along the net at which the ball is contacted.

post
    n. the standard that supports the net.

posture
    n. body position while performing a skill.

precontact position
    n. the floor location arrived at and the body positioning assumed before the ball arrives.

pump
    n. a play in which an attacker fakes spiking a quick set and then spikes, at the same location, a medium-height set.

push
    n. to lengthen a set; an attack where the player pistons his/her arm rather than swinging, "pushing" the ball across the net; an illegal lift.

quick
    n. a low, fast, inside set.

quick/shoot
    n. a play that includes both a quick set and a shoot set.

quick slide
    n. a quick attack that includes a two-footed takeoff and a broad jump along the net.

rally
    n. One series of play, from the service until the ball is dead.

read
    n. to determine what event will take place before it occurs; a blocking scheme in which the front-row players watch the setter in order to determine where to block; a back-court defensive scheme based on all players reading their opponents and their teammates.

ready position
    n. the flexed, yet comfortable posture a player assumes before moving to the point of contact.

rebound angle
    n. angle of the contact surface of the body at the moment of ball contact; commonly refers to forearm passing and hand position in blocking.

reception error
    n. a service reception error.

release
    n. a high set, usually delivered to the left sideline, that serves as an outlet when the play goes awry; a block pattern in which an outside blocker fronts the quick hitter as the middle double blocks on the sideline; the action of the ball leaving the setter's hands; the action of the setter moving toward the net.

reverse
    n. a combination in which the usual quick hitter attacks a play-set and the usual play-set hitter attacks a quick set.

reverse bump
    n. a desperation ball-handling technique sometimes necessary but seldom encouraged. It occurs when a player brings the hands together in front of the face, elbows bent. The ball is contacted in front of the face on the back of the forearms.

right-stack
    n. a commit-block scheme in which the right starts behind the middle in order to follow the crossing attacker.

roll shot
    n. a ball cleanly hit with the heel or palm of the hand.

rotate
    n. to advance on position in the line-up; a back-court defense in which the line defender moves near the block and the middle back moves behind the line defender.

rotation
    n. the players' locations on the court, according to the scorer.

safety
    n. a planned change in the blocking scheme used when the team confronts an attack it cannot cover.

scoop
    n. slang referring to the J stroke. The ball is played with the hands clasped together, the thumbs parallel and pointed up and the elbows bent.

seam
    n. the mid-point between two players.

serve
    n. one of the six basic skills used to put the ball in play. It is the only skill controlled exclusively by one player.

serve receive
    n. the tactical skill of directing the opponent's serve to the setter so that he or she can set. Forearm passing is the most common technical skill used to serve receive.

service ace
    n. a serve that hits the floor or causes the serve receiver to misplay the ball in such a manner that another player cannot make a second contact.

service error
    n. charged when the serve touches the net, fails to clear the net, lands out-of-bounds, touches the antenna or the server is called for a line violation, delay of service or rotational fault.

service reception error
    n. charged when the serve strikes the floor untouched, no teammate is able to make a second hit or the player is called for an illegal contact.

set
    n., v. the tactical skill in which a ball is directed to a point where a player can spike it into the opponent's court. Overhead passing is the most common technical skill used to set.

shag
    v. to retrieve balls that have been played, missed or terminated in a drill and returning them to the leader of the drill.

shot
    n. any directed individual attack attempt.

side-out
    n. occurs when the receiving team successfully puts the ball to the floor against the serving team or when the serving team commits an unforced error and the receiving team thus gains the right to serve.

skill
    n. the coordinated, effective function required by a specific motor task.

skip step
    n. resembles a hop. The feet are moved simultaneously from one position to a new balanced position. Primarily used to describe a common footwork pattern in ball handling.

specialize
    n. to concentrate efforts on one part of the game.

spike
    n., v. to hit the ball forcefully into the opponents' court.

spike coverage
    n. players on the attacking team assume low ready positions around their attacker in order to to retrieve rebounds from the opposing blockers.

spiker
    n. the attacker.

split block
    n. a double block that leaves a space between its blockers.

shadow of the block
    n. the area behind the block into which the opposing spikers cannot hit the ball hard.

shallow
    n. near the net.

shank
    n. a severely misdirected forearm pass.

shoot
    n. a low, fast set to an attacker who is away from the setter.

shuffle
    n. a footwork pattern in which the feet do not cross each other; used to cover short distances.

sidespin
  n. the resulting movement of the ball when spin is imparted in the horizontal plane, usually due to striking the ball off-center, causing the ball to follow a somewhat sideways path.

slide
  n. an attack approach that includes a last moment move along the net.

soft block
  n. a technique in which the blocker angles his/her hands backward in order to deflect the ball and slow its speed.

spike
  n. an attack to put the ball to the opponent's floor with force.

soft block
  n. a technique in which the blocker angles his/her hands backward in order to deflect the ball and slow its speed.

spike
  n. an attack to put the ball to the opponent's floor with force.

stack-man
  n. a commit-block scheme in which the follower is assigned to block one attacker only.

stack-read
  n. a commit-block scheme in which the follower determines, by reading the setter, whom he blocks.

step-around
  n. a one-footed slide in which the attacker moves around the setter.

step-in
  n. a one-footed slide in which the attacker moves toward the setter.

step-out
  n. a one-footed slide in which the attacker moves away from the setter.

stuff
  v. to block the ball to the floor.

stuff block
  n. a ball that has been blocked to the floor.

swing
  n. to move from one sideline to the other, usually in approaching to attack; a type of offense that uses the swing approach.

switch
  n. to change positions on the court.

tandem
  n. a combination in which one player attacks immediately behind another.

tape
  n. the top of the net.

target
  n. the player who is intended to receive the ball in any given play. The target can be the setter who is in the correct court position, an opponent who is designated to receive a serve or a spiker who is waiting to receive a set.

target area
  n. the court position where the target players should be.

technique
  n. the mechanics of a skill.

telegraph
  n. to show one's intention to the opponents.

terminal attack
  n. a spike or tip that has been successfully executed so that it is unplayable by the defensive team.

terminal contacts
  n. contacts which lead directly to points or side-outs for the contacting team. Kills and ace serves are all terminal contacts. An unforced error such as a net violation is also considered terminal.

three

n. a shoot that is attacked between the setter and the left sideline.

throw

n. a lift, usually characterized by a throwing motion.

thug

n. descriptive slang for a player who can terminate under adverse circumstances.

tip

n. 1. one-handed placement or redirection of the ball with the fingers-v. 2. to place or redirect the ball with the fingers of one hand.

tomahawk

n. descriptive slang for a reverse bump.

topspin

n. the resulting movement of the ball when spin is imparted in the vertical plane in a forward direction, usually due to striking the ball and following through by snapping the wrist. A ball with topspin will drop faster than a ball with little or no spin.

toss

n. 1. a skill used to initiate the contact of service. 2. a skill used to duplicate the dynamics and trajectory of a pass, serve or set during a drill. Both hands should be used to impart less spin on the ball.

touch

n. 1. a player contacting the ball. -interj. 2. an exclamation made by a blocker to inform his/her backcourt defenders that he/she has contacted the ball.

touch block

n. a control block.

trajectory

n. the curve the ball takes on its path from one player to another.

transition

n. the change from defense to offense.

trap

n. 1. a set close to the net that gives the blocker the advantage. -v. 2. to concentrate the block on one hitter, ignoring another.

triple-block

n. a block formed by three players.

two

n. a medium-height set that is usually attacked near the center of the net. See also play-set.

underhand serve

n. a serving technique in which the ball is contacted at about waist height by the serving hand.

unforced error

n. an error committed by a player that is unrelated to the opponent's play. Touching the net, stepping over the center line and serving into the net are examples of unforced errors.

veer

v. to change direction sharply during a spike approach; see also break.

wing

n. the player located on the extreme right or left of the formation.

W

n. a serve-receive formation with three players in the front row, two in the back (in the shape of a "W").

X

n. a cross in which the middle attacks a front one and the right attacks a two to the left of the middle.

X series

See 51X.

zone block

n. when the blockers take away a significant portion of the defense back court in which the opposing spiker can hit by being in good blocking position relative to the opposing spiker.